Education, Aid and Aid Agencies

Also available in the Education as a Humanitarian Response Series

Education as a Global Concern, Colin Brock
Education and HIV/AIDS, Nalini Asha Biggs
Education and Minorities, Chris Atkin
Education and Reconciliation, Julia Paulson
Education, Refugees and Asylum Seekers, Lala Demirdjian

Also available from Continuum

Comparative and International Education, David Phillips and Michele
    Schweisfurth
Schools for the Future Europe, John Sayer and Lynn Erler

Education, Aid and Aid Agencies

Education as a Humanitarian Response

Zuki Karpinska

continuum

Continuum International Publishing Group
The Tower Building   80 Maiden Lane
11 York Road   Suite 704
London SE1 7NX   New York NY 10038

www.continuumbooks.com

British Library Cataloguing-in-Publication Data
A catalogue record for this book is available from the British Library.

ISBN: HB: 978-1-4411-1233-0
      PB: 978-1-4411-2632-0

Library of Congress Cataloging-in-Publication Data
Education, aid and aid agencies / edited by Zuki Karpinska.
   p. cm. – (Education as a humanitarian response)
Includes bibliographical references and index.
ISBN 978-1-4411-2632-0 – ISBN 978-1-4411-1233-0 –
ISBN 978-1-4411-5483-5 – ISBN 978-1-4411-1916-2
1. Education–Developing countries–Case studies. 2. Economic
development–Effect of education on–Case studies. I. Karpinska, Zuki.

LC2605.E2893 2012
370.9172'4–dc23
                                                   2011040412

Typeset by Newgen Imaging Systems Pvt Ltd, Chennai, India
Printed and bound in India

Contents

Series Editor's Preface   vii
Notes on Contributors   viii
Acknowledgements   xi
List of Abbreviations and Acronyms   xii

1   **Education, Aid and Agencies: A Global Overview**   1
Zuki Karpinska

2   **Global Aid Frameworks: Application of *INEE Minimum Standards* for Advocacy, Coordination and Quality Education Provision for Burmese Refugees in Thailand**   33
Fred Ligon, Tzvetomira Laub and Allison Anderson

3   **Donor Policies: The Evolution and Development of DFID's Commitment to Education in Fragile States (2000–10)**   51
Peter Colenso

4   **Leadership: Save the Children's Global Challenge**   71
Katy Webley

5   **Coordination: Education and the IASC Cluster Approach in the Ivory Coast**   90
Pilar Aguilar

6   **Relief to Development: Community-Based Education and State-Building in Afghanistan**   113
Sara Bowers Posada and Rebecca Winthrop

7 Crisis Prevention: DRR through Schools in India   130
   Debdutt Panda and John Abuya

8 Cross-Cutting Issues: Youth-Centred Programming for
   Palestinian Refugees in Lebanon   147
   Adona El-Murr

9 Conclusion   163
   Zuki Karpinska

Index   167

Series Editor's Preface

Underlying this entire series on *Education as a Humanitarian Response* is the well-known adage in education that 'if we get it right for those most in need we will likely get it right for all if we take the same approach'. That sentiment was born in relation to those with special educational needs within a full mainstream system of schooling. In relation to this series it is taken further to embrace not only the special educational needs of those experiencing disasters and their aftermath, whether natural or man made, but also to other groups who may be significantly disadvantaged. Indeed, much can be learned of the value to the provision of mainstream systems from the holistic approach that necessarily follows in response to situations of disaster. Sadly very little of this potential value is actually perceived, and even less is embraced. Consequently one of the aims of the series, both in the core volume *Education as a Global Concern*, and the contributing volumes, is to bring the notion of education as a humanitarian response to the mainstream, and those seeking to serve it as teachers, other educators and politicians. The situation of international aid and education is one in which this issue is clearly illustrated in terms of the frequent disconnect between education in emergencies and education for sustainable development. Zuki Karpinska has addressed this fundamental issue both in her valuable overview chapter and in her selection of sub-themes and authors for the contributions that follow. Key issues such as donor policy, coordination of inputs from agencies and leadership are addressed in relation to well-chosen examples from different parts of the world.

This particular contribution to the series, *Education, Aid and Aid Agencies*, also inherently illustrates problems of interaction between the three main components of scale in relation to educational provision, international, national and local. A greater understanding of the issue of scale should be at the forefront of thinking about the type of education we need to be fostering in order to be successful in meeting the challenge of sustaining the human and physical environment on planet Earth.

Colin Brock
UNESCO Chair in Education as a Humanitarian Response
University of Oxford, UK

Notes on Contributors

John Abuya is International Thematic Programmes Manager for ActionAid International, and was previously ActionAid's International Project Manager for the multi-country Disaster Risk Reduction through Schools (DRRS) Project. The project is being implemented in nine countries: Bangladesh, Nepal, India, Haiti, Malawi, Ghana, Kenya, the Democratic Republic of the Congo (DRC) and Zambia. Prior to that, John managed ActionAid's long-term development and emergency programmes as Programme Director (Kenya), acting Country Director (Malawi and Rwanda), Country Director (Burundi) and Director (Great Lakes Region, covering Burundi, Rwanda and DRC).

Pilar Aguilar is Senior Education Advisor at UNICEF, as well as the Capacity Development focal person in Education in Emergencies for both UNICEF and the Inter-Agency Standing Committee (IASC) Education Cluster. Pilar has worked to develop and improve systems for improving education in camps for refugees and internally displaced persons – such as UNICEF's 'Child Friendly Spaces' – and to establish and strengthen networks and coordination mechanisms – such as the Inter-Agency Network for Education in Emergencies (INEE) and the Education Cluster.

Allison Anderson is a non-resident fellow with the Center for Universal Education at the Brookings Institution, where she focuses on how quality education can help mitigate the impact of disasters and promote climate change adaptation and conflict resolution. Allison notably held the posts of the first Director of INEE as well as the INEE Coordinator for Minimum Standards. Prior to INEE, Allison worked with adolescents affected by conflict in Kosovo, Sierra Leone and Northern Uganda with the Women's Refugee Commission.

Sara Bowers Posada is Portfolio Manager at the Nike Foundation, funding projects that empower adolescent girls worldwide. She has worked on education and protection in countries including Zimbabwe, Uganda, Guatemala and Afghanistan. Sara has also designed and implemented education programmes in South Asia with Catholic Relief Services (CRS), including the

Partnership Advancing Community-Based Education in Afghanistan (PACE-A) programme.

Peter Colenso is Director, Investments, for the Children's Investment Fund Foundation. He was previously Head of the Human Development Group in the UK Department for International Development (DFID) Policy Division, leading DFID's policy and international work on education, health, nutrition and HIV/AIDS. Prior to that he was DFID's Head of Education. Peter has worked for the World Bank, the UN, the European Commission and NGOs in Africa, Asia and the Balkans. He has a Doctorate of Education from Sussex University.

Adona El-Murr is a facilitator, trainer and mentor working with teams, individuals and business units in leadership development and change management through her business, Key Distinctions. With a background in the humanitarian sector, she worked in the United Nations Relief and Works Agency for Palestine Refugees (UNRWA) Lebanon Field Office from 2005 to 2008.

Zuki Karpińska is a specialist in education policy and planning in situations of instability and a dedicated member of INEE and the Education Cluster Working Group.

Tzvetomira Laub is INEE Coordinator for Minimum Standards. She coordinates and provides support to INEE individual and organizational members to promote, implement, train on and institutionalize the *INEE Minimum Standards* handbook. Previously, Tzvetomira worked as a consultant and project coordinator at the Watchlist on Children and Armed Conflict and supported the UN Security Council negotiations on Resolution 1882. She has also worked with CARE and the Balkan Sunflowers in Kosovo.

Fred Ligon is Senior Advisor with World Education Thailand, and served as Director from 1999 to 2010, managing a refugee training programme implemented in nine refugee camps on the Thailand–Burma border. Until 2011, Fred was a member of the INEE Working Group on Minimum Standards and has developed an Internal Reflection Tool for use in monitoring the application of the *INEE Minimum Standards* in refugee and migrant education projects in Thailand within the two projects he manages. Previously, Fred worked with education projects in Nigeria, Indonesia and Cambodia.

Debdutt Panda is Coordinator, Programme Support and Education Rights on the International Education Team for ActionAid. Prior to taking up this position, he led the DRRS project in India as part of ActionAid India. He also worked with the Commonwealth Education Fund India, a joint initiative of ActionAid, Save the Children and Oxfam working in sixteen countries on the Education for All Campaign. Before joining the development sector, he contributed numerous articles on education, health and other developmental issues to leading national dailies in India. Debdutt holds a PhD in Political Science from Jawaharlal Nehru University, New Delhi, India.

Katy Webley is Director of Policy and Programme Development for Save the Children UK's Ethiopia Programme, a department that includes the Education, Health, Nutrition and Livelihoods thematic teams, the Emergencies Unit and the Everyone Campaign Team. She was Save the Children UK's Head of Education from 2005 to 2010, and Education Advisor from 2003 to 2005. Previous roles have included working as Education Manager in South Sudan, Primary Education Teacher Trainer in Eritrea and Primary Teacher in the United Kingdom.

Rebecca Winthrop, Senior Fellow and Director of the Center for Universal Education at the Brookings Institution, is an international expert on global education, particularly in contexts of armed conflict. She works to promote equitable learning issues for young people in developing countries. She advises governments, foundations, and corporations on education and development issues, and provides guidance to a number of important education policy actors. Prior to joining Brookings in June 2009, Rebecca spent 15 years working in the field of education for displaced and migrant communities, most recently as Head of Education for the International Rescue Committee (IRC).

Acknowledgements

This volume is dedicated to Dr Margaret Sinclair, whose matchless wisdom, productivity and commitment have set the bar for education-in-emergencies planners. She is both role model and rock star to me, and countless others.

I wish to sincerely thank Prof Colin Brock for offering me and the other contributors the opportunity to share the stories told within this volume.

I also thank the staff at Bloomsbury and Continuum for their patience and guidance throughout the process of its development process.

Most of all, I thank the dedicated individuals who authored the case studies here compiled. I underscore that the stories told are their own, and do not necessarily reflect the opinions of others in the institutions about which they write. The authors have bravely contributed their personal accounts of education-in-emergencies planning – warts and all – so that others may learn from their experiences.

With gratitude,
Zuki Karpinska, editor

List of Abbreviations and Acronyms

ABEC	Afghanistan Basic Education Consortium
ADRA	Adventist Development and Relief Agency
AKF	Aga Khan Foundation
ALNAP	Active Learning Network for Accountability and Performance
AUB	American University of Beirut
BCG	Boston Consulting Group
BMWEC	Burmese Migrant Workers Education Committee
BPL	below poverty line
CAAC	Children and Armed Conflict
CAP	Consolidated Appeals Process
CBE	Community-Based Education
CBO	Congressional Budget Office
CCSDPT	Committee for Coordination of Services to Displaced Persons in Thailand
CEPE	Certificat d'Etude Primaires Elementaires
CLG	Community Life Guards
CNO	Centre, North and West of Côte d'Ivoire
CPIA	Country Policy and Institutional Assessment
CRC	Convention on the Rights of the Child
CRS	Catholic Relief Services
CSOs	Civil Society Organizations
DAC	Development Assistance Committee
DFID	Department for International Development
DIPECHO	Disaster Preparedness, European Community Humanitarian Office
DMOSS	Direction de la Mobilisation et des Oeuvres Sociales Scolaires
DREN	Directions Regionaux d'Education National
DRR	disaster risk reduction

DRRS	Disaster Risk Reduction through Schools
ECD	early childhood development
EFA	Education For All
EFA-FTI	Education For All Fast Track Initiative
EiE	education-in-emergencies
EPT	Education pour Tous
FAO	Food and Agricultural Organization
GCPEA	Global Coalition to Protect Education from Attack
GFDRR	Global Facility for Disaster Reduction and Recovery
GMR	Global Monitoring Report
GSE	Groupe Sectoriale Education
GVM	Gramya Vikas Mancha
HE	higher education
HFA	Hyogo Framework for Action
HSCC	Hazard Safety Cadet Corps
IASC	Inter-Agency Standing Committee
IEP	Inspection de l'Education Primaire
IM	information management
INEE	Inter-Agency Network for Education in Emergencies
INGO	international NGO
IRC	International Rescue Committee
ISDR	International Strategy for Disaster Reduction
KCT	Key Challenge Team
KNU	Karen National Union
LFO	Lebanon Field Office
MDG	Millennium Development Goal
MEN	Ministère de l'Education Nationale
MESRS	Ministère de l'Enseignement Supérieur et de la Recherche Scientifique
METFP	Ministère de l'Enseignement Technique et de la Formation Professionnelle
MGNREGA	Mahatma Gandhi National Rural Employment Guarantee Act
MINUCI	UN Mission in Côte d'Ivoire
MOE	Ministry of Education
MRM	Monitoring and Reporting Mechanism on Children and Armed Conflict
NAVTSS	National Association of Vocational Training and Social Services

NCERT	National Council for Education Research and Training
NGOs	nongovernmental organizations
OCHA	UN Office for Coordination of Humanitarian Affairs
OECD	Organization for Economic Cooperation and Development
PACE-A	Partnership for Advancing Community-Based Education in Afghanistan
PRSP	Poverty Reduction Strategy Paper
PVA	Participatory Vulnerability Analysis
RFA/RFP	Request for Applications/Proposals
SC Members	Save the Children Members
SMART	Specific, Measurable, Achievable, Realistic, Timebound
SMC	school management committee
SRSG	Special Representative to the Secretary General
SSA	Sarva Shiksha Abhiyan
SVA	Shanti Volunteer Association
TEP	Teacher Education Programme
TVET	technical and vocational education and training
UN	United Nations
UNDP	UN Development Programme
UNESCO	UN Educational, Scientific and Cultural Organization
UNFPA	UN Population Fund
UNHCR	UN High Commission for Refugees
UNICEF	UN Children's Fund
UNOCI	UN Operation in Côte d'Ivoire
UNRWA	UN Relief and Works Agency for Palestine Refugees
USAID	United States Agency for International Development
WG	Working Group
WHO	World Health Organization

Education, Aid and Aid Agencies: A Global Overview

Zuki Karpinska

1

Chapter Outline

Introduction	1
Humanitarian aid	4
The humanitarian aid industry and its critics	6
Global debates about aid and their corresponding frameworks	8
Coordination of humanitarian aid	13
What is education in emergencies?	15
Advocacy for education in emergencies	18
Current state of education in emergencies	21
An introduction to the themes discussed in this volume	25

Introduction

Emergency humanitarian responses are immensely expensive. The challenge of providing aid to countries and populations affected by conflict and natural disaster makes generating funds a critical first step. It is perhaps no surprise that public and government responses to aid agency fundraising appeals are driven by images of intense and immediate human suffering.

Yet, this funding is not only necessary for setting up tents or feeding programmes: funds are also needed to replace destroyed school buildings to provide a space for learning; for training available, literate adults to teach children in the midst or aftermath of chaos; and for gathering displaced communities to warn them of the dangers of nearby landmines and the risk of HIV/AIDS in the camps where they may remain for decades. It also costs money to plan: to work with affected populations to assess their needs and then to go through the usually laborious process of applying for funding.

This, however, is not a book about resources. It is rather a book about convincing those with money that education provision is imperative in areas where disaster has struck, conflict has traumatized both children and adults and political or climactic factors are all too predictive of future crises. In short, this is largely a book about advocating for education's place in emergency response.

Historically, in crisis situations requiring humanitarian aid interventions, some 'donors have taken the view that it is sufficient to keep emergency-affected people from dying and to look after their physical health' (Sinclair, 2001: 4). This perception – that education is not immediately necessary in times of crisis – is changing, largely thanks to the individuals who have contributed case studies to this volume. Education is now on the humanitarian aid map. Slowly, and probably far too slowly, funding is being made available for education programming in the most challenging of contexts.

This series – *Education as a Humanitarian Response* – focuses on education provision in emergency situations, defined as areas and populations affected by natural disaster or armed conflict. This particular volume – *Education, Aid and Aid Agencies* – discusses international support for teaching and learning interventions through a series of case studies, which present the rationale for funding and programming decisions as perceived by the very individuals responsible. Among the authors are the architects of the main coordination and networking mechanisms (and 'household names'!) within the education-in-emergencies (EiE) community. Among the aid agencies whose strategies and programmes comprise these case studies are the leading operational and funding institutions within the arena of education as a humanitarian response. Among the stories told are detailed descriptions of the often mediocre sources of information available to these decision-makers and how the authors translated this information into strategies for action.

This introductory chapter lays down a foundation for considering the relationship among education provision, the underlying structures of the industry of humanitarian assistance and the institutions that form the global aid community. It also anticipates key themes of current relevance to education programming for crisis-affected populations, which will be further discussed in the case studies within this volume.

In order to situate the relationship between and among education, aid and aid agencies, I begin by considering the concept of humanitarian aid, which has traditionally focused on immediate response to sudden crises, and of its relationship to development assistance, which has been regarded as a series of interventions designed to move a country forward on a path of steady social and economic progress. This extended point of departure – including discussion of global aid frameworks and coordination mechanisms – is necessary in order to position the education sector within the wider arena of international aid structures and their evolution, both theoretical and institutional.

The fundamental question of this entire volume is whether education is a 'life-sustaining', 'life-saving' humanitarian response on par with the provision of food and water, healthcare and shelter. In this regard, the most crucial development for putting education squarely on the humanitarian aid map has been a network of decision-makers, planners and field practitioners committed to education provision in the harshest of circumstances. The formation and the subsequent exponential growth and activity of this professional and advocacy network has led to increased attention to education as a humanitarian response, both within the institutions that house the networks' members as well as in the broader humanitarian aid structures. And some of the people who have played the most visible roles within this network have written the case studies in this book.

The description of the inadequate funding environment for education in emergencies in this introductory chapter is necessarily brief. The status quo is simple: the education sector consistently falls short of its funding appeals. It is far more interesting to consider how this shortage might be rectified. The chapter highlights several important developments of late that have not only resulted from targeted advocacy for education in emergencies but may also be used for further advocacy. Successful advocacy equals more money for programming.

The chapter ends with a synopsis of the themes within the arena of education as a humanitarian response that are illustrated through case studies in successive chapters in this volume. The themes include donor policies, illustrated by a case of the evolution of a commitment to 'fragile states'; coordination, illustrated by a case of country-level joint agency advocacy for education in emergencies; and crisis prevention, illustrated by a local-level disaster risk reduction project. It is hoped that the case studies presented here will illuminate the breadth of contextual factors that planners attempt to reflect in every strategy, programme and activity. The case studies portray institutional and contextual parameters that shape the planning processes of the illustrious contributors to this volume: the policy-makers, analysts, technical advisors and field staff engaged with education provision in emergencies. And each case study tells the story of an approach to education provision in crisis contexts, as told by the individuals responsible for decision-making. Importantly, this volume is about the leadership of these authors, and the people and the institutions with whom they engage to shape their thinking about education in emergencies. Rather than financial resources, advocacy is the central theme of this book: advocacy that takes place within the structures of the humanitarian aid industry.

Humanitarian aid

Humanitarian aid refers to the technical, human, material and financial resources provided to disaster- and conflict-affected populations in order to relieve immediate suffering and – increasingly – to rebuild affected areas. The need for this aid is growing:

> Globalization and the increasingly interconnected world in which we live means that disasters often have a global impact. Pandemics spread rapidly through air travel. Economic shocks in one region spread through commodity price increase and loss of remittance flows. Conflict does not respect borders, and spillover from conflict-affected areas contributes to regional destabilization and refugee flows. Migration and changing employment patterns will contribute to vulnerability in unexpected ways, with the potential to create new security threats. (DFID, 2011: 11)

The quotation above indicates that crises may have disastrous – and uncontainable – consequences in countries that are unable to cope on their own. Those concerned with the planning of aid delivery are not only directly burdened with the responsibility of saving the lives of crisis-affected populations, but also indirectly burdened with the responsibility for preventing a recurrence of the crisis. There is no telling what later impacts will result from oversights now.

Humanitarian aid has been originally viewed as a short-term enterprise intended to relieve immediate suffering in crisis situations whereas development aid has been viewed as a longer-term enterprise intended to improve living conditions in low- and middle-income countries. The dividing line between these forms of aid is often unclear. Many institutions separate them into 'rigid compartments for "humanitarian" and "development" aid, each of which are governed by different rules and often managed by different departments of the same donor agency' (INEE, 2010a: 28). At which point – or points – does humanitarian aid leave off and development begin? And how does this divide shape perceptions of the imperative to provide education in all contexts to all populations?

The roots of modern-day humanitarian action date back over 150 years. On 24 June 1859, French and Austrian armies fought the Battle of Solferino, in what is now Italy. Henri Dunant, a Swiss citizen, organized the local population to provide assistance to the wounded soldiers without regard to their national affiliation. His memoir inspired the 1863 founding of the International Committee of the Red Cross. The following year, the first Geneva Convention was ratified, thereby formalizing the concept of humanitarian aid, and establishing the principles of neutrality, impartiality, independence and universality of aid provision.

While modern humanitarian assistance may be, and usually is, provided by a government to its own citizenry, the focus of this volume is on aid offered by 'external' aid agencies, such as international nongovernmental organizations (NGOs), United Nations (UN) aid bodies, foreign government donors and foundations. The establishment of a plethora of aid institutions followed that of the Red Cross. By the Second World War, many of the largest NGOs in existence today had begun some form of service to the needy. Shortly thereafter, UN agencies were established as transnational, nondenominational enterprises in the development/humanitarian aid enterprise. In the ensuing decades, aid provision increased exponentially, developing into a multibillion-US$ industry. This industry has created a new profession: the aid worker. The total number of humanitarian aid staff, with the vast majority being local recruits who work in their own crisis-affected countries, is estimated at over 200,000 (DFID, 2011: 4). The authors of the case studies in this volume are all aid professionals – decision-makers, planners, analysts and/or programme managers – who have unique stories to tell about their experience in the education sector of humanitarian response.

The Organization for Economic Cooperation and Development's (OECD) Development Assistance Committee's (DAC) *Statistical Reporting Directives* define humanitarian aid as:

> Assistance designed to save lives, alleviate suffering and maintain and protect human dignity during and in the aftermath of emergencies. To be classified as humanitarian, aid should be consistent with the humanitarian principles of humanity, impartiality, neutrality and independence. . . . [This] includes: disaster prevention and preparedness; the provision of shelter, food, water and sanitation, health services and other items of assistance for the benefit of affected people

and to facilitate the return to normal lives and livelihoods; measures to promote and protect the safety, welfare and dignity of civilians and those no longer taking part in hostilities and rehabilitation, reconstruction and transition assistance while the emergency situation persists. (OECD, 2007: 20)

This quotation highlights several of the concepts that are explored within this text: the idealism inherent in the above, the use of a discourse particular to the humanitarian aid industry and the notable absence of education in many lists of humanitarian interventions.

Education is inherently a multi-year process, but aid interventions in emergency contexts are not always planned with an eye toward the longer term – that is, recovery and reconstruction. A 2004 overview of the scope of education provision in emergency situations found that humanitarian actors have long engaged in teaching and learning, skills building and creation of safe spaces for children in certain emergency settings (Women's Commission, 2004). Yet, only recently has 'education' surfaced as an explicit generic concern to donor agencies as a potentially routine part of humanitarian response; of the billions spent annually on aid, the proportion of funding for education remains small.

Although often-vilified, aid institutions devote significant time and resources to planning interventions designed to alleviate immediate suffering while simultaneously strengthening the coping strategies of individuals, households and communities. This should include formal education. The authors who have contributed to this volume are strong advocates for education in emergencies within their own institutions and beyond. Operating within the wider parameters of the humanitarian aid industry, their decisions and those of their colleagues have shaped how aid agencies interact with the education sector.

The humanitarian aid industry and its critics

The term 'humanitarian' has a highly idealistic, altruistic connotation.

The notion that 'being humanitarian' and 'doing good' are somehow inevitably the same is a hard one to shake off. For many people, it is almost counter-intuitive to have to consider that humanitarian action may also have a dark side which compromises as well as helps the people whose suffering it seeks to assuage. (Slim, 1997: 244)

A central tenant of humanitarian aid should be to 'do no harm' (Anderson, 1996). However, the humanitarian aid industry as a whole has been widely criticized as sometimes doing more harm than good: for allocating the majority of resources to the highest-profile disasters (Vaux, 2006); for creating dependency and thus perpetuating the cycle of poverty (Sharp & Devereux, 2004); for increasing numbers of refugees with the 'lure of aid' and for fuelling conflict (Barber, 1997); for ignoring the 'humanitarian imperative' of neutrality and following Western political interests in the allocation of aid (Olsen et al., 2003); for lack of 'sustainability'; and for undermining longer-term development objectives (Macrae, 2001). Much has also been written about the fallacy of the aid discourse: of the very notion that one may plan to 'do good' (see, e.g., Sachs, 1992; Crush, 1995). These criticisms are often, but not always, accurate.

Importantly, such aid critiques frequently grossly overestimate the potential of policies and subsequent programmes to 'do good,' and then criticize the outcomes. It is nearly impossible to isolate the effects of a particular intervention: experimental conditions are hard to reproduce outside of laboratories. Any gain for, or any harm to, a given population in which development or aid projects take place is the result of complex, specific and dynamic contexts in which many factors – in addition to, or instead of, a given intervention – have a part. These contexts are formed by the nexus of geographical, sociocultural, economic and political factors, among others. Planning to 'do good' requires intimate knowledge of these contexts, the input and enthusiasm of all stakeholders involved and adequate funding.

There is no question that many development and humanitarian aid programmes – like public policy in general – have had poor results. In a paper on the 'unintended, unanticipated and unwelcome consequences of public policy', Perri 6 (2008) asks – given the volume of writing on such criticisms of policies – 'whether their very ubiquity makes the question of their causes and the vulnerability of human action to them, any longer a very interesting question' (p. 1). This volume is thus far less interested in documenting successes and failures of humanitarian aid than it is with describing aid planning and how it relates to the policy contexts in which it occurs.

It is possible to acknowledge that there are many problems with the humanitarian aid industry as a whole but to still consider external aid support a worthwhile enterprise. 'Numerous poor, marginalized and disempowered people in many parts of the world would be far worse off if *all* short-and longer-term development efforts cease. . . . Critique alone is inadequate' (Simon, 2007: 208, 214).

Global debates about aid and their corresponding frameworks

The provision of humanitarian aid to crisis-affected countries has strong roots in the normative ideal that there are 'universal' human rights that apply to all. According to the rhetoric, every man, woman and child has the right to freedoms such as speech and to services such as health. De Waal (2010) even makes the argument that there is now an 'idea of a *right* to humanitarian assistance' (p. S134). Likewise, the 'universality' of the moral imperative to provide assistance to the disadvantaged is a fundamental tenet of the aid industry.

Yet, some of these Western-centric rights have been questioned as antithetical to Islamic (see, e.g. Cerna, 1994) and other cultures. External aid agencies, predominantly headquartered in Europe and the United States 'desire to spread development, democracy, and human rights, and to join a peace-building agenda that aspires to create stable, effective, and legitimate states' (Barnett, 2005: 733). The 'universality' of each of these concepts may be questioned in turn; however, the important point to take forward is that the humanitarian industry was shaped by Western values that are viewed by policy-makers as applicable to all.

Cornwall and Brock (2005) comment that the terms used in the planning of aid 'are never neutral. They acquire meaning as they are put to use in policies. And these policies, in turn, influence how those who work in development think about what they are doing' (p. 1056). It is thus important to reflect on the language and principles of aid that form the structural and policy frameworks for development assistance and for humanitarian relief. As relief aid increasingly takes a longer-term view, development rhetoric increasingly influences humanitarian planning. These discourses are not stagnant but have undergone sufficient changes that the aid rhetoric may be divided into 'trends'.

For instance, human capital theory, which posits that investment in education is key to economic growth, is a discursive trend that still has currency today with institutions such as the World Bank, over half a century since its first use to frame development assistance policy (Robertson et al., 2007: 52).

A more recent trend is that of rights-based approaches to development. Although hardly uniform in conception and practice (Cornwall & Nyamu-Musembi, 2004), rights-based approaches emerged in the mid-1990s as the antithesis of needs-based development: aid is viewed as fulfilment of rights rather than the distribution of charity. Rights-based approaches are based on humanitarian principles, human rights frameworks and/or international law. These may include the principles of universal entitlement and inalienability of rights; of the indivisibility, interdependence and equal status of rights in upholding the dignity of all persons; of non-discrimination and of the equality of all persons; of the right to participation of all persons in development; and of accountability, both on the part of duty-bearers (those responsible for ensuring rights, usually States – with or without the assistance of the international aid community) and of rights-holders (UNICEF/UNESCO, 2007). In essence, rights-based approaches aim to recognize and honour the agency of populations affected by crisis, or poverty, leading to greater 'ownership' of development and aid processes and 'empowerment' of affected populations.

Another such trend is that of aid effectiveness. Due to the vast sums involved, donors have begun to demand greater 'accountability' for allocated funds in the form of quantifiable targets for aid interventions. 'The period of the late 1980s led to a closer focus on [aid] efficiency and managing for results, and . . . closer public scrutiny of foreign assistance by Western publics' (Bermingham et al., 2009: 132). Simultaneously, aid discourse attached great importance to the idea of aid as a partnership with mutual responsibilities, rather than the traditional donor–recipient relationship. According to the rhetoric, aid funding must be consistent with the priorities of aid-receiving governments in order to achieve desired results on the part of donors, and – to the extent possible – this aid should be channelled through aid-receiving government institutions. Such 'principles' of aid delivery have been enshrined in the Paris Declaration on Aid Effectiveness (2005) – country ownership, alignment with government priorities, harmonization of donor investments, results-based management, mutual accountability – and the follow-up Accra Action Agenda (2008).

The ideals espoused within these frameworks are frequently difficult to achieve in crisis contexts. Working with and through aid-receiving government offices is predicated on sufficient capacity of these offices to absorb and disburse funding: for example, adequate levels of financial management skills, existence of budgetary infrastructure, safeguards to minimize corruption, ability to meet the stringent donor reporting requirements. In instances where crisis-affected government offices are non-existent or lack these capacities, donor institutions tend to fund NGOs directly, as they often have long histories of activity in a given development or chronic–crisis context and have the requisite infrastructure to channel funding into desired programme activities. This 'parallel aid system' may bypass government structures altogether, and governments may sometimes be unaware of activities operating in their own countries.

The development/humanitarian aid focus on poverty reduction – another aid trend – is evidenced by its primary importance as the first of the Millennium Development Goals (MDGs). Arguably the most significant contemporary global aid framework is the action plan of the September 2000 UN Millennium Summit. Its list of MDGs provides numerical, time-bound targets that signatory countries have pledged to try to achieve by 2015. As the focus of this volume is the education sector within the humanitarian aid industry, most pertinent to this research are MDG 2 – 'achieve universal primary education' – and MDG 3 – 'promote gender equality and empower women' in terms of, inter alia, access to schooling opportunities (UN, 2000). There is growing recognition that education may be key to reducing poverty, not only due to its link to increases in individual income, but also due to its possible role in conflict prevention. 'While the economic justifications of education as human capital have not disappeared, it is increasingly recognized that economic growth is undermined by conflict and that a broader understanding of education's role in promoting tolerance, peace and prosperity needs to be examined . . .' (Novelli, 2010: 453). In fact, there is a strong argument that education is central to achieving the rest of the MDGs, as well: that education has been shown to improve maternal health (MDG 5) and reduce child mortality (MDG 4) and that education is key to the transfer of knowledge about disease prevention (MDG 6) and environmental sustainability (MDG 7) (UNESCO, 2010a).

The central global aid framework for those concerned with education is the Dakar Framework for Action The UN Children's Fund (UNICEF), UN Development Programme (UNDP), UN Educational, Scientific and Cultural Organization (UNESCO), UN Population Fund (UNFPA) and the World Bank were the convening agencies of the Education For All (EFA) movement borne of a 1990 conference in Jomtien, Thailand. As a result of the conference, representatives of 155 countries and over 150 institutions declared a commitment to universalize primary education and drastically reduce illiteracy by the new millennium. Ten years later, of course, none of this had happened. Thus, a second meeting of similar delegates was held in Dakar in 2000: the World Education Forum. The Dakar Framework for Action acknowledged the need for special attention to education in situations of instability (UNESCO, 2000). Goal 2 of the so-called EFA targets specifically indicates that 'children in difficult circumstances' are included in the target of achieving universal primary education by 2015.

With the 2015 deadline for achievement of both the MDGs and the EFA targets soon approaching, it is now commonly accepted that there is no evidence to suggest that sufficient progress is being made for all signatory states to reach the goals by 2015. Jansen (2005) situates his criticism of such goals and targets within the longer spectrum of attempts to implement international normative frameworks. He writes, 'what is striking about the serial commitment to target setting is that each new landmark conference over the decades acknowledges that the targets have not been met, and then proceeds immediately to set another round of targets' (p. 369).

It is important to note that many global aid frameworks offer little, if any, guidance on how the targets or principles therein may be achieved. In his article on the implications of setting numerical goals within the EFA targets, Goldstein (2004) argues that the Dakar Framework for Action contains 'no indication of the problematic nature of such measurements' (p. 8) and that it would be much more useful to adopt the broad aims of the framework and devise strategies to meet them. Goal 4, which calls for a 50 per cent improvement in adult literacy rates, is particularly awkward, as many countries have literacy rates of over 66.7 per cent and thus could not possibly improve these to over 100 per cent (Colclough, 2005).

Critiques of normative frameworks such as the MDGs and the Dakar Framework for Action generally acknowledge that the reliance on numerical 'targets' may actually undermine the very aims that these goals are intended to achieve (Goldstein, 2004). For instance, in its rush to achieve universal primary education, the Kenyan government abolished school fees in 2003 and could not cope with the overnight increase in enrolment; without the requisite concomitant increase in the teaching force and education infrastructure, the quality of education suffered (Sifuni, n.d.). Laird (2005) questions the consequences of setting such 'universal' global goals, positing that the 'Western' values and focus on measurable indicators embodied by the MDG targets lead to the 'imposition of interventions upon an unconsidered and un-scrutinised social setting' (p. 464). Much like the 'universality' of human rights, universal application of these frameworks is contested. Such 'one-size-fits-all development recipes stripped of any engagement with context or culture, politics, power or difference, does violence to the very hope of a world without poverty' (Cornwall & Brock, 2005: 1058).

Yet, these frameworks shape the aid programmes that are developed and implemented, as they define the parameters of what planners and practitioners should aim to achieve. Interestingly, the MDG and EFA targets are so overwhelmingly embedded in humanitarian aid discourse and planning – often as an aid to fundraising – that some critiques of these goals do not question their development and imposition, but – rather – their ambition (see, e.g., Clemens et al., 2006). The focus on universal primary education without regard to the need for concomitant quantitative and qualitative improvement in education at secondary and tertiary levels is increasingly considered to be unfortunate, given the need for teachers at the primary level as well as educated personnel for the wider economy.

It is important to note that there are different modalities for funding in times of crisis – different methods of channelling financial resources, which constitute aid frameworks in and of themselves. These are concisely described in the *INEE Reference Guide on External Education Financing* (INEE, 2010a). Some funding modalities provide support to specific projects or activities, at the donor's discretion, while some provide leeway for an aid-receiving government to allocate the funds according to its own priorities within its budget or a sector within the budget. For humanitarian action, two of the most important fundraising mechanisms are the Flash Appeal and the Consolidated Appeals Process (CAP). These UN-managed funding appeals are designed to attract bilateral and multilateral financial resources for humanitarian action in crisis situations. Country-level actors jointly decide on affected-population needs in the different aid sectors and draw up prioritized plans: in the immediate aftermath of an emergency, a Flash Appeal is issued for urgent needs; if longer-term humanitarian aid is required, an annual CAP is prepared. The CAP, in particular, may be viewed as an umbrella, national-level coordination mechanism for all humanitarian agencies and their planned actions.

Further to donors such as Western governments and multilateral agencies such as World Bank, new categories of aid actors are emerging. 'Post-Cold War interventionism has led to a massive increase in both peacekeeping and development assistance directed to conflict and post-conflict countries resulting in a massive expansion of humanitarian and development personnel and an expansion of the nature of the activities that these organizations engage in' (Novelli, 2010: 455). As private organizations and military forces have increasingly become major actors in humanitarian aid provision, the 'traditional' categories of operational, aid providing institutions – the UN and its agencies, the Red Cross and Red Crescent Movement and NGOs – are expanding (DFID, 2011: 4). Foreign military bodies as well as for-profit corporations and contractors are changing the aid landscape, and these actors do not necessarily attempt to adhere to global aid frameworks such as the

Paris Declaration or the Accra Action Agenda, nor do they participate in joint appeals processes.

Coordination of humanitarian aid

The global aid frameworks mentioned in the previous section, as well as many other such frameworks, provide standardization of approaches, common goals and shared principles among the many aid actors. To an extent, these policy documents serve to coordinate aid approaches of aid agencies who adopt them. Coordination in humanitarian aid may be defined as 'the systematic utilization of policy instruments to deliver humanitarian assistance in a cohesive and effective manner' (Minear et al., 1992: 3). In other words, the aim of coordination requires standardization in terms of policies and procedures for provision of aid programming. Yet, this is an elusive goal for the humanitarian aid industry. As Sommers (2004) writes,

> Why is the act of co-ordinating humanitarian and post-conflict reconstruction activities so difficult? In principle, it should be simple and straightforward: the work by different actors in sectors such as education should fit together and complement each other. It does not make sense for them to overlap or leave gaps in service. Working as a team to address the collective needs of people recovering from tragedy and disaster seems the appropriate, logical and humanitarian thing to do. (p. 17)

In 2005, the UN Emergency Relief Coordinator had commissioned the Humanitarian Response Review, a report that was to identify 'gaps' in contemporary approaches to international assistance in crisis situations and to provide recommendations for the improvement of these approaches. The report recommended that the Inter-Agency Standing Committee (IASC) institute a cluster approach 'as a way of addressing gaps and strengthening the effectiveness of humanitarian response through building partnerships' between UN agencies, the International Red Cross and Red Crescent Movement and NGOs (UN/HRSU, 2008). The approach envisions that '[p]artners work together towards agreed common humanitarian objectives both at the global level (preparedness, standards, tools, stockpiles and capacity-building) and at the field level (assessment, planning, delivery and monitoring)' (ibid.). Various UN agencies were thus to be designated Global Cluster Leads, for example the World Health Organization (WHO) would – and now does – lead the Health Cluster; essentially, the approach assigns a given UN agency to be in charge of coordination of humanitarian response, should a natural or man-made disaster occur anywhere in the world.

The cluster approach is to eliminate 'turf battles, empire-building, overlapping and conflicting mandates and ad hoc arrangements' (Reindorp & Wiles, 2001: 8), themes identified from past studies of complex emergencies in a study on UN agency coordination in humanitarian response. Improving coordination among humanitarian aid institutions and government bodies within the crisis context is thus a main objective of the cluster approach. In the first phase of the planned two-phase evaluation of the cluster approach commissioned by the IASC, Stoddard et al. (2007) found that the 'approach has improved efforts to identify and address gaps within sectoral programming in humanitarian response in the field' and 'marginally improved' collaboration between UN agencies and international NGOs (p. 1). The findings of this early study must be considered cautiously, as it was undertaken when only fourteen countries (ibid.) had activated the cluster approach, compared to over triple that number today. The second-phase evaluation, concluded in 2010, stated that investments in the cluster approach are 'beginning to pay off as the benefits generated by the cluster approach to date already slightly outweigh its costs and shortcomings' (Steets et al., 2010: 10). What is interesting about this statement is that a cost-benefit analysis methodology was not used in the research.

A key responsibility of clusters is information management, as set forth in the *IASC Operational Guidance on Responsibilities of Cluster/Sector Leads and [UN Office for Coordination of Humanitarian Affairs] OCHA in Information Management.* The term 'information management' (IM) refers to the design and application of tools, systems and structures to determine what information to share, with whom, for what purpose and how. IM focuses on the facts and figures of a situation: the kind of data and information collected using needs assessments and/or monitoring and evaluation (M&E) studies.

Strong IM, carried out in support of coordination processes in a given emergency, will ensure that the relevant actors are working with the same or complementary information and baseline data, and that this information is as relevant, accurate and timely as possible. Properly collected and managed data during emergencies are, furthermore, beneficial for early recovery and later development and disaster preparedness activities (IASC, 2007: 1).

However, data collection in emergency, post-conflict and post-disaster situations is notoriously difficult. Obstacles include issues relating to logistics, physical security, ethics, political implications of activities in rapidly changing environments and the technical challenges of working with mobile populations and populations with unusual demographic compositions (Schlecht & Casey, 2006). Poor, destroyed or non-existent records render baseline compilation for the purposes of comparison problematic, if not impossible. Analysing and compiling data into useful information to share among aid actors also requires scarce temporal, technical and financial resources. Yet, information is 'the foundation on which decision-making for a coordinated and effective response is based' (IASC, 2007: 1).

Humanitarian aid coordination, therefore, operates at several interconnected levels: that of global aid frameworks – including principles and funding mechanisms – as well as national policies; global-, country- and sub-country-level coordination mechanisms such as the cluster approach; and shared collection of and access to national- and local-level data. Education provision in (post-)crisis situations – the focus of this volume – occurs within these aid structures and their inputs.

What is education in emergencies?

Education in emergencies is concerned with the issues surrounding education provision for populations affected by conflict or natural disaster. Although not the first to use 'education in emergencies' as an umbrella term, Sinclair (2001) wrote in her seminal chapter in a larger text on refugee education that 'the term "education in emergencies" increasingly serves as shorthand' for a range of structured activities – including schooling – designed 'for and with' crisis-affected populations (p. 4). A host of other terms have been used to describe the field and its subcategories, including 'education in emergencies, chronic crises and early reconstruction' (INEE, 2004); 'education and fragile states' (Kirk, 2007); 'education in crisis situations' (Burde, 2005); 'emergency education' (Kagawa, 2005); 'education and conflict' (Davies, 2004; Tomlinson & Benefield 2005); 'education and (post-)conflict' (Rose & Greeley, 2006); and 'education for reconstruction' (Arnhold et al., 1996).

The scope of the field of education in emergencies is vast. Implementation of education programmes in crisis contexts requires human resources who are skilled (or at least conversant) in sectors such as logistics, in order to procure and transport teaching and learning and construction materials; shelter/construction, to design, situate and erect safe learning spaces; curricula, to ensure quality teaching and learning; policy, to guide government and other education provider planning and resource allocation; data collection, collation and analysis, to determine needs of the affected populations and monitor programmatic outcomes; community mobilization, to harness community technical and material resources for education institution establishment or management; training – of teachers, school management committee (SMC) members and teacher trainers; negotiation – between and among education service providers, communities and parties to conflict, among other expertise. And this list is also incomplete. It is impossible to possess expertise in all of these areas, and all-but-impossible to address each of these considerations in every programmatic activity offered. However, those concerned with education in emergencies agree that addressing each of these factors in turn is necessary for the provision of education in all contexts – including those affected by disaster and conflict.

> The 'universal' right to education has been articulated in a number of internationally ratified human rights instruments and is protected by international law (see e.g. UNESCO, 2010b). For instance, Article 26 of the Universal Declaration of Human Rights (1948) states: 'Everyone has the right to education'; to this end, access to education should be free of charge 'at least in the elementary and fundamental stages'. The right to education is also enshrined in the Convention Relating to the Status of Refugees (1951), International Covenant on Economic, Social and Cultural Rights (1966) and in the almost universally ratified Convention on the Rights of the Child (CRC) (1989), among other such rights frameworks. The right to education spelled out under these agreements is of greater, not lesser, importance in emergencies, as it gives a lifeline of hope. The [CRC] covers persons up to the age of 18, but does not, of course, suggest that the right to education be denied from that age on, and other human rights documents do not have this limitation. In fact, many crisis-affected young people in their twenties attend primary or secondary school because their education was delayed, or disrupted by war or instability in their country, or because this is the only constructive activity open to them in refugee or IDP camps, or simply because higher education, which is included in the Convention, essentially caters to young adults. (Sinclair, 2002: 34)

Some humanitarian aid institutions follow mandates – or written strategies or policies – to address educational provision. Most international education-providing institutions are primarily concerned with 'basic education': 'a combination of indispensable competencies, knowledge, skills and attitudes that serves as the foundation of any individual's lifelong learning' (Pigozzi, 1999), generally acknowledged to be learned at the primary and – lately – junior secondary level of schooling. Few of these institutions have a clear policy to support secondary education, even though their mandate as child-focused organizations requires attention to the needs of adolescents up to age 18. They often ignore tertiary education (a notable exception being UNESCO, which frequently lacks funding for substantive backing of higher education). However, 'education' encompasses not only schooling at primary, secondary and tertiary levels, but also early childhood development (ECD), technical and vocational education and training (TVET), literacy programmes and life-skills education, such as HIV/AIDS or landmine awareness training. Some of these programmes have long been provided – under different names – as part of emergency response, while other forms of so-called non-formal education have only recently become a focus of education aid providers.

Arguably, the groundwork for the field of education and emergencies dates back 15 years to the publication of Machel's (1996) seminal report *Impact of Armed Conflict on Children,* which highlighted the plight and needs of children affected by conflict – the result of 2 years of research by the then-UN Secretary General's appointed expert on the issue. Several years later, Machel (2001) used the phrase 'fourth pillar' of humanitarian response, referring to the life-saving imperative of educational provision in emergency situations, along with the other pillars of aid: food and water, shelter and healthcare.

Donors have historically been loath to fund education as an emergency response, questioning its categorization as a life-saving intervention. Is education as immediately life-sustaining and life-saving as the other core humanitarian aid sectors? If education is defined broadly, then the answer is yes (see, e.g., Women's Commission, 2004). Education programmes allow for the immediate, and immediately needed, dissemination of important messages, such as landmine awareness, disaster risk reduction and/or HIV/AIDS sensitization. Education programmes can provide physical protection from the dangers of a crisis environment. When a child is in a safe learning environment he or she is less likely to be sexually or economically exploited or exposed to other risks, such as voluntary recruitment into an armed group. Importantly, there is another reason to engage in education immediately: ignoring the education sector can result in severe psychosocial problems later; a faster return to normalcy may reduce trauma. Also, missing out on school in times of conflict or natural disaster may keep children out of school permanently, resulting in longer-term grievances and return to conflict.

The 'fourth pillar' argument and similar oft-cited arguments in the 'field' of education and emergencies have been widely accepted, but more research is needed to validate such claims. For instance, in a World Bank published text, Buckland (2005) claims that 'the post-conflict reconstruction environment is the best of times and the worst of times, both an opportunity and a constraint' for educational reform (p. 25). The battle-cry 'build back better' is certainly heard in aid circles. Rose and Greeley (2006) – in a paper prepared for the OECD/DAC's Fragile States Group – claim that educational provision often acts as a 'barometer' of a government's commitment to its citizenry; this claim may be supported anecdotally, but it would prove difficult to quantify. Another claim is Bush and Saltarelli's (2000) – published by UNICEF's Innocenti Research Centre – argument that education in situations of instability has 'two faces', that education may be used to promote peace and stability through its structures and content or that it may entrench existing inequalities and foster conflict. This claim, that education is often harnessed for negative objectives during conflict, is strongly supported by scholarly work, such as Davies (2004), Kirk (2007) and Harber (2004). The publishing institutions of these influential arguments have been highlighted in this paragraph to show that the literature of education in emergencies is still mostly grey, funded by donor institutions and aid agencies.

Advocacy for education in emergencies

Education became a recognized humanitarian aid sector through coordinated and strategic advocacy. In their seminal work on transnational advocacy networks, Keck and Sikkink (1998) describe them as 'forms of organization characterized by voluntary, reciprocal, and horizontal patterns of communication and exchange', supporting and strengthening the voice of advocates who 'plead the causes of others or defend a cause or proposition' (p. 8). Such networks "frame' issues to make them comprehensible to target audiences, to attract attention and encourage action' (Keck & Sikkink, 1998: 90). Advocacy is here defined as a process by which an institution or coalition attempts to influence or change policy and practice through the strategic use of 'policy analysis, research, and the channeling of information' (Hudson, 2001). Such advocacy ranges from raising awareness – through networking, capacity building or campaigning – to direct action (Unerman & O'Dwyer, 2005).

The network for those concerned with advocating for education as a humanitarian response is the Inter-Agency Network for Education in Emergencies (INEE). INEE 'is a global, open network of nongovernmental organizations, UN agencies, donors, practitioners, researchers and individuals from affected populations working together within a humanitarian and development framework to ensure the right to education in emergencies and post-crisis reconstruction' (INEE, n.d.). INEE is neither a UN agency nor an NGO; it is a professional network of educational stakeholders in – or those interested in – situations of instability. INEE members subscribe to the following notion:

> Children have a right *to* education (access to quality education), they have rights *in* education (a non-discriminatory environment based on respect and the best interest of the child); and they gain rights *through* education (the ability to make informed choices concerning their lives and to participate as citizens in the world). (Anderson et al., 2011)

INEE has its roots in the EFA movement. During the 2000 World Education Forum's Strategy Session on Education in Emergencies in Dakar, the representatives of UN agencies and other institutions proposed that a permanent network be established to improve collaboration and coordination among institutions and to strengthen existing networks (INEE, n.d.). INEE was officially founded at the November 2000 follow-up Inter-Agency Consultation in Geneva, convened by UNHCR, UNICEF and UNESCO. There were one hundred representatives from thirty institutions who attended this first 'consultation' conference (INEE, 2008). Due to individual rather than institutional efforts, a small group of highly placed educational planners within these UN agencies and international NGOs expanded the network exponentially over the past decade, and INEE currently boasts over 7,000 members (INEE, n.d.). INEE members donate their time and ask their institutions to donate resources to explore and share findings on issues related to education planning and practice in situations of instability. INEE is the largest such network concerned with education in emergencies.

The structure of INEE is relatively simple, considering the scope of its activities. The INEE Secretariat currently comprises only a few paid employees, all housed in different member organizations: International Rescue Committee (IRC) in New York; UNICEF in New York; UNESCO in Paris; and UNHCR in Geneva (INEE, n.d.). The Secretariat is largely responsible for maintaining INEE's voluminous website and coordinating and monitoring INEE's activities. The Secretariat reports to the INEE Steering Group, which consists of representatives of NGOs, UN agencies and the World Bank, all of whom are supported by their respective institutions. The Steering Group sets the agenda for the network, facilitates its activities and administers its budget. Apart from semi-annual meetings of its Steering Group and Working Groups, most of INEE's activities are conducted through online communication among members.

Upon its establishment, INEE's agenda was to:

> Share knowledge and experience; promote greater donor understanding of education in emergencies; advocate for education to be included in humanitarian response; make teaching and learning resources available as widely as possible; ensure attention to gender issues in education in emergency contexts; document and disseminate best practices; and move toward consensual guidelines on education in emergencies. (INEE, 2008)

To pursue this agenda, the work of INEE is undertaken by its two Working Groups (WGs) – the WG on Minimum Standards and the WG on Education and Fragility – as well as individual Task Teams devoted to producing guidance on a particular topical issue, such as gender. The WGs are permanent bodies convened by the Steering Group, and the Task Teams are output-oriented groups convened by INEE members in response to a perceived need. For instance, the now-dissolved Teacher Training Task Team compiled 'best practice' guides and support materials to serve as a one-stop resource kit for practitioners concerned with teacher training in situations of instability; as with all INEE products, this resource is available free of charge on the INEE website as well as on CD-ROM. In addition to the work of the WGs and the Task Teams, the INEE website (http://www.ineesite.org) offers links to a wide range of information and resources, including practitioner-oriented 'good practice guides' and scholarly articles.

According to a seminal article by Wilensky (1964), the professionalization of an occupation entails establishing a body of full-time practitioners (often, in the beginning, from other fields); creating training programmes; forming a professional association; developing certification for the new profession; and, finally, establishing a code of ethics. Within the EiE community, many of these steps have already been undertaken. INEE published and widely disseminated the 2004 *INEE Minimum Standards* handbook (an authoritative guide on education programme planning and implementation in and after emergencies) and its 2010 update (INEE, 2004; 2010: see Chapter 2). INEE has also collected and documented so-called best practices from a number of institutions concerned with educational provision in situations of instability, and either published these or posted them on the INEE website. *INEE Minimum Standards* trainings, as well as a range of other trainings by member institutions, strive to systematize practice and the application of 'lessons learned'. Higher education institutions – such as the University of Nairobi – are developing postgraduate courses in education in emergencies. Vaux (2006) observes that these efforts are paying off: 'On the ground there is a sense of greater professionalism, and more confidence in knowing what needs to be done, at least in terms of techniques and standards' (p. 242).

One of the greatest successes of INEE member lobbying efforts has been the establishment of an IASC cluster for education. Initially, education was not a sector in which the cluster approach was to be used (Adinolfi et al., 2005). Yet, following the ad hoc adoption (UN/IASC, 2006) of the then-only-theoretical cluster approach in Pakistan in the aftermath of the October 2005 earthquake, during which the collapse of school buildings made the education sector a highly visible priority in the reconstruction process, aid agencies created a 'cluster' for education. Using this and other evidence on the importance of education in emergencies, the INEE lobby – as well as individual agency efforts – attained their goal. Education was approved as a permanent cluster by the IASC in late 2006, but – due to budgetary constraints – the Global Unit was not created until early 2008; at the country and sub-country levels, however, education clusters were functioning prior to this date despite the lack of global leadership (Stoddard et al., 2007). Worldwide, the Education Cluster is led by UNICEF and co-led by the Save the Children Alliance, and is the only cluster that is not exclusively led by a UN agency. The Global Education Cluster Unit is housed in Geneva.

Current state of education in emergencies

Education is the poor neighbour of a humanitarian aid system that is underfinanced, unpredictable and governed by short-termism. It suffers from a double disadvantage: education accounts for a small share of humanitarian appeals, and an even smaller share of the appeals that get funded. The EFA Global Monitoring Report's best estimate is that in 2009, humanitarian aid for education amounted to US$149 million – around 2% of total humanitarian aid. Just over one-third of requests for aid to education receive funding. The chronic underfinancing behind these data leaves children in conflict areas and displaced populations out of school. (UNESCO, 2011: 19)

As stated earlier, education – as a sector – falls far behind the core humanitarian responses of food and water, health and shelter. What is interesting is that country-level humanitarian actors operational in education – in their awareness of the second or third tier position of education in donor policies – adjust their budgets accordingly. These actors, cognizant of donor reluctance to fund education as a humanitarian response, routinely ask for only a small piece of the aid pie and receive even less. Importantly, only a handful of DAC donors – Canada, Denmark, Japan, Norway, Sweden – have humanitarian policies that explicitly include education as a first line of response or that refer to education as part of their humanitarian policy (Brannelly et al., 2009). Further, many donors to education in emergency situations are reluctant to contribute to recurring costs – such as teacher salaries or facilities upkeep – favouring tangible investments – such as school construction or provision of teaching and learning materials, or one-off teacher training.

In 2008, INEE sponsored a Policy Roundtable on *Education Finance in States Affected by Fragility* hosted by the European Commission in Brussels, Belgium. The event was organized by the INEE Working Group on Education and Fragility, which was established in early 2008 as an inter-agency mechanism to coordinate diverse initiatives and catalyse collaborative action on education and fragility. Major points of discussion from the event (INEE, 2008: 1) included the need for simple, flexible and quick funding mechanisms; issues of trust gaps between donors and recipient countries; the role of new sources of fragility, such as the global recession, in driving fragility and potentially reducing funding to education; lack of capacity and knowledge at country level to make effective choices about utilization of financing modalities; challenges of shadow alignment; and uncertainty over the role of civil society in financing of education in fragile contexts. These concerns are, of course, ongoing. They are also not limited to the education sector. Although the relationship among donors, aid-receiving governments and international institutions with on-the-ground presence in crisis-affected areas often seems like an us-against-them battle, most aid actors are equally frustrated by the problems of aid provision in crisis-affected areas.

However, for supporters of education provision in crisis contexts, several recent developments augur increased attention to education in emergencies and associated international action (i.e. funding) for its provision.

Reform instituted in January 2011 of a key funding mechanism will hopefully make it easier for conflict-affected countries to access needed resources. The Global Partnership for Education, formerly the Education For All Fast Track Initiative (EFA-FTI), is a multi-donor programme that provides technical and financial support for development of education sector plans for governments, helps finance the implementation of these plans in countries struggling to meet the EFA targets and provides a 'seal of approval' to encourage resourcing from other donors. The reform of 2010 has, inter alia, streamlined application processes and relaxed stringent documentation prerequisites that had made it unfeasible for governments with limited capacity – such as those experiencing conflict and insecurity – to benefit from education support through this major funding source.

The most recent issue of the *Education for All Global Monitoring Report* (GMR) (UNESCO, 2011) – a widely disseminated annual UNESCO publication that tracks progress of the achievement of EFA targets – was dedicated to exploring the relationship between education and conflict. Through grim statistics, the 2011 GMR illustrates the impact of armed conflict on education. About 42 per cent of out-of-school children reside in conflict-affected low-income countries; the average duration of violent conflict in these countries is twelve years, the entire primary and secondary school cycle; only six days of military spending by high-income countries would provide the estimated US$16 billion of external assistance necessary to meet EFA targets (UNESCO, 2011: 2–3). The report also draws attention to the potential negative impacts of education on conflict: 'Intra-state armed conflict is often associated with grievances and perceived injustices linked to identity, faith, ethnicity and region' (UNESCO, 2011: 16). These include disparities in access to education, which widen the gap between the rich and poor; the entrenchment of prejudice and intolerance through politicized curricula; the failure of education systems to prevent drop-out, whether caused by poor quality or other barriers to school progression; and/or raising unrealistic hopes that education will lead to better employment opportunities in countries ravaged by war. In addition, the 2011 GMR highlights the human rights abuses that are rife in conflict-affected contexts – including sexual attacks on students, destruction of school buildings and forcible exclusion of girls from education opportunities – that serve to prevent access to education through an environment of fear. The publication's focus on conflict raises the profile of the challenges of education provision in 'fragile states', which may lead to much-needed increases in external funding.

On 9 July 2010, the UN General Assembly passed a resolution on education in emergencies, in which it reaffirmed the right to education in all contexts, called for an end of under-financing of the sector in emergency situations and urged states to provide quality education in all stages of emergency response. The resolution is the crowning achievement of years of advocacy on the part of the aid agencies and governments concerned with education provision for crisis-affected populations. Its significance lies in UN members' recognition of education as a humanitarian response, as well as of the frameworks developed under the aegis of INEE: most notably the *INEE Minimum Standards* and the *INEE Guidance Notes on Safer School Construction*, which are mentioned by name. EiE advocates may almost consider the resolution an international testimony of appreciation for a decade's worth of work.

A high-profile report of human rights violations against children has – in July 2011 – provided greater weight to attacks on schools that occur in areas of violent conflict. UN Monitoring and Reporting Mechanism on Children and Armed Conflict (MRM) was established by UN Security Council Resolution 1612 in 2005 (see also Resolution 1882). The MRM addresses six 'grave violations': (a) killing and maiming of children; (b) recruitment into or use of children in armed forces; (c) rape/grave sexual abuse of children; (d) abduction of children; (e) attacks against schools or hospitals; and (f) denial of humanitarian access for children. The Office of the Special Representative to the Secretary General (SRSG) on Children and Armed Conflict (CAAC) compiles reports from countries in which the MRM has been instituted and ensures that the report findings are presented to a working group of the UN Security Council. It is intended that these reports prompt action by the UN Security Council and other relevant policy actors, resulting in pressure upon conflicting parties to halt violations against children. The MRM is triggered, or put in motion, in countries where armed forces are known to recruit children, carry out sexual violence against children and/or kill or maim children. This list of triggers has now been expanded to include attacks against schools: a major advocacy coup for those concerned with education in emergencies.

Perhaps ironically, the strongest advocacy point for education provision in emergency contexts may be the growing recognition on the part of Western governments that 'development policy "abroad" and security at "home" are directly linked' (Novelli, 2010: 453). Conflicts and disasters result in population movements borne out of fear and poverty; donor governments are taking notice of the correlation between lack of livelihood opportunities and refugee flows to Western countries (or, more ominously, terrorist attacks on Western soil). With crisis-affected populations consistently ranking education highest on their list of needs, the failure to provide meaningful education services in 'fragile states' may become a security concern for Western governments.

An introduction to the themes discussed in this volume

Subsequent chapters in this volume each extract a theme from those discussed in this overview of education, aid and aid agencies, and present a case study of decision-making by influential individuals operating within their own understandings of the culture of their institutions and within the parameters of the wider humanitarian aid industry. Although the introduction and conclusion for all of these chapters was written by me, the meat and heart of each chapter – the case study of decision-making by those responsible – is by the eminent aid professionals listed below.

As discussed, a number of global aid frameworks exist to provide a shared, standardized vision of the aims and principles of development and humanitarian assistance. Arguably, the *INEE Minimum Standards* handbook constitutes the most comprehensive global aid framework for those concerned with educational services provision in situations of instability. For more than two decades, the ongoing conflict between the military government in Burma and Burmese ethnic minorities has forced more than 150,000 people to seek refuge in Thailand. Fred Ligon of World Education, with the support of Tzetomira Laub and Allison Anderson, examines the application of the *INEE Minimum Standards* to advocate for, strategize, coordinate, design and provide educational services to the Burmese refugees who had fled to the neighbouring country following days of shelling and fighting in the summer of 2009. Within the discussion of the theme of global aid frameworks, the chapter introduces the important concepts of institutionalization and contextualization – two strategies for making sense of overarching 'universal' goals at a local level.

Chapter 3 discusses the development process of donor policies, specifically the evolution and development of the UK Department for International Development's (DFID) commitment to education in 'fragile states'. Fragility has become a hot topic in donor circles, the understanding of which helps provide a foundation for donor engagement in crisis-affected contexts. This case study of donor policy describes the progression of DFID's concern with fragile states in general, then looks specifically at education provision in fragile states, before examining patterns of UK expenditure. Next, Peter Colenso considers whether and how this commitment translated into increased investment in DFID's country programmes through analysis of overall levels of investment in DFID's country programmes, and then in the education sector specifically. Finally, the case study examines in greater detail why DFID decided to scale-up support to education in fragile states, citing three reasons: (i) to focus UK resources on where they could best accelerate progress toward the MDGs, (ii) to promote broader processes of peace-building, state-building and poverty reduction in fragile states, (iii) to protect UK national interests.

The case study in Chapter 4 highlights the importance of leadership, both individual and institutional, in advocacy and programme development for education in emergencies. Save the Children is the world's leading independent organization for children, whose vision is a world in which every child attains the right to survival, protection, development and participation. In 2005, Save the Children decided to focus its energies, for the first time, on a 'Global Challenge'. The purpose of the challenge was to bring together the twenty-nine national Save the Children organizations to work collectively on a single issue, to build ambition, raise dramatic funds and deliver greater change for children. The Global Challenge was later renamed as *Rewrite the Future*, with a series of strategies to address four broad objectives – children's access to education, the quality of education, protection of school children and financing of education. In a first-person narrative account, Katy Webley describes the process of development of this seminal initiative, the success of which would cement Save the Children's leadership role in the field of education in emergencies.

Chapter 5 describes the intent of the coordinating role of the Education Cluster. The UN/IASC Humanitarian Reform and the adoption of the cluster approach have changed the way that humanitarian response in situations of instability is led and coordinated. The Ivory Coast, a country emerging from repeated civil strife over the past decade, has benefited from two aid agency coordination bodies in the past few years: an education sector working group, and – since January of 2011 – the Education Cluster. This case study, by Pilar Aguilar, illustrates the success of external aid agencies in raising the profile of education in emergencies within government structures. It also provides a case of the translation of global coordination guidance into the Ivorian context.

One of the tensions in the field of education in emergencies is the immediacy of the need for humanitarian relief versus the long-term nature of education processes. In cases where conflict has been particularly protracted and widely destructive, post-conflict recovery presents both problems as well as major opportunities, especially within the education sector. During this window, normally rigid Ministries of Education may be open to change, providing an opportunity in which to transform and improve education systems. In response to the great inequities of the Afghan education system during the Taliban era, USAID invested in a five-year community-based education project as a major pillar of education recovery. Sarah Bowers Poseda and Rebecca Winthrop present a case study of the spectrum of aid phases – from acute emergency to development – and examine the challenges of programme planning within a shifting and dynamic (post-)crisis context.

A growing concern for humanitarian aid planners is that of crisis prevention: how education aid programming may be used in order to minimize the damage in the aftermath of conflict and natural disaster. Since 2005, ActionAid International has devoted much of its human and financial resources to disaster risk reduction (DRR), a group of interventions designed to reduce vulnerability to natural disasters. Disasters due to natural hazards like floods, drought and earthquakes destroy the lives of more than 300 million people every year; the increasingly apparent impacts of climate change further aggregate the risk of disaster. Importantly, in most cases, the poorest and most vulnerable are affected first and are hit hardest. By building community resilience and by helping people adapt to climate change, the impact of future disasters can be reduced. Debdutt Panda and John Abuya describe the rationale behind ActionAid's pioneering focus on DRR, drawing on the organization's experience in Assam and Andhra Pradesh, India.

Finally, aid agencies acknowledge that a range of additional themes, so-called cross-cutting issues, must be embedded in all aid interventions so as to 'do no harm', as well as to take advantage of programming opportunities to address concerns of vital importance in addition to the goals of a particular project. Chapter 8 presents a case study of a project whose very beneficiary group constitutes a cross-cutting issue – youth – for Palestinian refugees in Lebanon. It is often forgotten that education in emergencies is not limited to interventions for primary-school-aged children. Adona El-Murr, who had worked with Palestinian refugees in Lebanon, presents a skills-training project in which the primary beneficiaries – as well as 'partners' in planning – are young adults. The project was driven by former and present staff of the UN Relief and Works Agency for Palestine Refugees (UNRWA), who designed its activities to address the educational needs of young people as well as to build their capacity for community development and activism. The case study shows how the commitment of the many actors involved in this youth-focused pilot project may have positive long-term impacts beyond those envisioned by project planners.

The educational comparativist Michael Crossley is fond of repeating that 'context matters', by which he refers to the need for thorough understanding of geo-socioeconomic-political factors and awareness of the unique circumstances created by the combination of these factors. Not only do local conditions matter, but so do personalities, institutions and global aid structures. The case studies provided in this volume show how these contexts affect a particular agency's approach to a broader issue within the sphere of humanitarian aid. The particular circumstances in which aid interventions take place affect the manner in which aid funding is allocated and aid projects are implemented.

Context does matter. Greatly. And so does funding. Greatly. Access to reliable information about contextual factors coupled with effective relationships with and among stakeholders, including – and perhaps most importantly – affected populations, lead to sound advocacy arguments for those with funding. And thus, perhaps, make it possible to 'do good'.

Key questions

- How has the wider humanitarian aid industry shaped conceptions of education in emergencies?
- Is education a 'life-sustaining', 'life-saving' humanitarian response on par with provision of food and water, healthcare and shelter?
- In what ways has advocacy for education in emergencies affected the growth of the sector?
- What are the challenges of education provision in situations of instability?

Further reading

Cahill, K. M. (ed.) (2010), *Even in Chaos: Education in Times of Emergency.* New York: Fordham University Press and the Center for International Humanitarian Cooperation.

An accessible, edited volume of essays and case studies by global leaders and field practitioners, addressing such topics as the right to education, the *INEE Minimum Standards,* child protection, attacks on education and national curricula.

INEE (2010a), *INEE Reference Guide on External Education Financing.* New York: INEE.

An excellent, easy-to-use handbook explaining the various funding modalities and types of donor agencies, including a useful glossary of terms.

Sinclair, M. (2002), *Planning Education in and After Emergencies*. Paris: UNESCO, International Institute for Educational Planning.

A seminal guide to policy and planning for education in emergencies structured around the principles of good practice, offering guidance not only for the provision of formal schooling but also for the so-called non-formal arena of peace and conflict resolution education.

UNESCO (2011), *Education for All Global Monitoring Report. The Hidden Crisis: Armed Conflict and Education*. Paris: UNESCO.

The annual report on progress towards the EFA goals, focusing on the harm caused by violent conflict with regard to access to and quality of education as well as donor failures to address these specific challenges in light of education's potential for building peace.

References

Adinolfi, C., Bassiouni, D., Lauritzsen, H. F. and Williams, H. R. (2005), *Humanitarian Response Review*. United Nations: New York and Geneva.

Anderson, A., Hoffman, J. and Hyll-Larsen, P. (2011 forthcoming), 'The right to education for children in emergencies'. *Journal of International Humanitarian Legal Studies* 2(1).

Anderson, M. (1996), *Do No Harm: Supporting Local Capacities for Peace through Aid*. Boston, MA: Collaborative for Development.

Arnhold, N., Bakker, J., Kersh, N., Mcleish, E. and Phillips, D. (1998), *Education for Reconstruction: The regeneration of educational capacity following national upheaval*. Oxford: Symposium Books.

Barber, B. (1997). 'Feeding refugees, or war? The dilemma of humanitarian aid'. *Foreign Affairs* 76(4), 8–14.

Barnett, M. (2005), 'Humanitarianism transformed'. *Perspectives on Politics* 3(4), 723–40.

Bermingham, D., Christensen, O. R. and Mahn, T. C. (2009), 'Aid effectiveness in education: why it matters'. *Prospects* 39, 129–45.

Blaikie, P. (2000), 'Development, post-, anti- and populist: a critical review'. *Environment and Planning A* 32(6), 1033–50.

Brannelly, L., Ndaruhutse, S. and Rigaud, C. (2009), *Donor's Engagement – Supporting Education in Fragile and Conflict-Affected States*. Paris: International Institute for Educational Planning.

Buckland, P. (2005), *Reshaping the Future: Education and postconflict reconstruction*. Washington, DC: World Bank.

Burde, D. (2005), *Education in Crisis Situations: Mapping the field*. Washington, DC: Creative Associates/USAID.

Bush, K. D. and Saltarelli, D. (2000), *The Two Faces of Education in Ethnic Conflict: Towards a peacebuilding education for children*. Rome: UNICEF Innocenti Research Centre.

Cerna, C. (1994), 'Universality of human rights and cultural diversity: implementation of human rights in different socio-cultural contexts'. *Human Rights Quarterly* 16(4), 740–52.

Clemens, M. A., Kenny, C. J. and Moss, T. J. (2007), 'The trouble with the MDGs: confronting expectations of aid and development success'. *World Development 35*(5), 735–51.

Colclough, C. (2005), 'Rights, goals and targets: how do those for education add up?' *Journal of International Development 17*, 101–11.

Crossley, M. (1999), 'Reconceptualising comparative and international education'. *Compare 29*(3), 249–67.

Cornwall, A. and Brock, K. (2005), 'What do buzzwords do for development policy? A critical look at "participation", "empowerment" and "poverty reduction"'. *Third World Quarterly 26*(7), 1043–60.

Cornwall, A. and Nyamu-Musembi, C. (2004); 'Putting the "rights-based approach" to development into perspective'. *Third World Quarterly 25*(8), 1415–37.

Crush, J. (ed.) (1995), *Power of Development*. London: Routledge.

Davies, L. (2004), *Education and Conflict: Complexity and chaos*. London: RoutledgeFalmer.

de Waal, A. (2010), 'The humanitarians' tragedy: escapable and inescapable cruelties'. *Disasters 31*(S2), S130–7.

DFID. (2011), *Humanitarian Emergency Response Review*. London: DFID. Retrieved 20 July 2011 from www.dfid.gov.uk/emergency-response-review.

Goldstein, H. (2004), 'Education for all: the globalization of learning targets'. *Comparative Education 40*(1), 7–14.

Harber, C. (2004), *Schooling as Violence: How schools harm pupils and societies*. Oxford: Taylor & Francis.

Hudson, A. (2001), 'NGOs' transnational advocacy networks: from "legitimacy" to "political responsibility"'. *Global Networks 1*(4), 331–352.

IASC. (2007*), Operational Guidance on Responsibilities of Cluster/Sector Leads and OCHA in Information Management*. Geneva: OCHA.

INEE. (n.d.) http://www.ineesite.org.

INEE. (2004), *Minimum Standards for Education in Emergencies, Chronic Crises and Early Reconstruction*. Retrieved 31 July 2011 from http://www.ineesite.org/minimum_standards/MSEE_report.pdf.

INEE. (2010a), *INEE Reference Guide on External Education Financing*. New York: INEE.

INEE. (2010b), *Minimum Standards for Education: Preparedness, Response, Recovery*. INEE. Retrieved 31 July 2011 from http://www.ineesite.org/uploads/documents/store/Minimum_Standards_2010_eng.pdf.

INEE Working Group on Education and Fragility. (2008) *INEE Policy Roundtable: Education finance in states affected by fragility. Outcome Report*. New York: INEE.

Jansen, J. D. (2005), 'Targeting education: the politics of performance and the prospects of "Education For All"'. *International Journal of Educational Development 25*, 368–80.

Kagawa, F. (2005), 'Emergency education: a critical review of the field'. *Compare 41*(4), 487–503.

Keck, M. and Sikkink, K. (1998), *Activists Beyond Borders: Advocacy networks in international politics*. Ithaca, NY: Cornell University Press.

Kirk, J. (2007), 'Education and fragile states'. *Globalisation, Societies and Education 5*(2), 181–200.

Laird, S. E. (2005), 'International child welfare: deconstructing UNICEF's country programmes'. *Social Policy & Society 4*(4), 457–66.

Machel, G. (1996), *Impact of Armed Conflict on Children. Report of the Expert of the Secretary General of the United Nations*. New York: United Nations and UNICEF.

— (2001), *The Impact of War on Children: A Review of Progress since the 1996 United Nations Report on the Impact of Armed Conflict on Children*. Paris: UNESCO.

Macrae, J. (2001), *Aiding Recovery? The crisis of aid in chronic political emergencies*. London: Zed Books.

Minear, L., Chelliah, U. B. P., Crisp, J., Mackinlay, J. and Weiss, T. (1992), *United Nations Coordination of the International Humanitarian Response to the Gulf Crisis 1990–1992*. Occasional Paper 13. Providence, RI: The Thomas A. Watson Jr. Institute for International Studies, Brown University.

Novelli, M. (2010), 'The new geopolitics of educational aid: from Cold Wars to Holy Wars?' *International Journal of Educational Development 30*, 453–9.

OECD. (2010), *DAC Statistical Reporting Directives*. DCD/DAC(2010)40/REV1. Paris: OECD.

Olsen, G. R., Carstensen, N. and Hoyen, K. (2003), 'Humanitarian crises: what determines the level of emergency assistance? Media coverage, donor interests and the aid business'. *Disasters 27*(2), 109–26.

Perri 6. (2008), 'When Forethought and Outturn Part: A Conceptual Framework for Understanding Unintended, Unanticipated and/or Unwelcome Consequences of Public Policy'. Seminar paper. 'Paradoxes of Modernization: Unintended Consequences of Public Policy Reforms' ESRC Public Services Programme, Oxford Internet Institute and DPIR Public Policy Unit. 4 March 2008.

Pigozzi, M. (1999), *Education in Emergencies and for Reconstruction: A developmental approach*. New York: UNICEF.

Reindorp, N. and Wiles, P. (2001), *Humanitarian Coordination: Lessons from recent field experience*. A study commissioned by the Office for the Coordination of Humanitarian Affairs (OCHA). London: Overseas Development Institute.

Robertson, S., Novelli, M., Dale, R., Tikly, L., Dachi, H. and Alphonce, N. (2007), *Globalisation, Education and Development: Ideas, actors and dynamics*. UK: DFID.

Rose, P. and Greeley, M. (2006), *Education in Fragile States: Capturing lessons and identifying good practice*. DAC Fragile States Group, Service Delivery Workstream, Sub-Team for Education Services. Paris: OECD.

Sachs, W. (ed.) (1992), *The Development Dictionary: A guide to knowledge as power*. London: Zed Press.

Schlecht, J. and Casey, S. (2006), 'Challenges of collecting baseline data in emergency settings'. *Forced Migration Review 29*, 68–70.

Sharp, K. and Devereux, S. (2004), 'Destitution in Wollo (Ethiopia): chronic poverty as a crisis of household and community livelihoods'. *Journal of Human Development 5*(2), 227–47.

Sifuni, D. N. (n.d.), 'The illusion of universal free primary education in Kenya'. *Wajibu: A Journal of Social and Religious Concern*. Issue 20. Retrieved 31 July 2011 from http://africa.peacelink.org/wajibu/articles/art_6901.html.

Simon, D. (2007), 'Beyond antidevelopment: discourses, convergences, practices'. *Singapore Journal of Tropical Geography 28*, 205–18.

Sinclair, M. (2001), 'Education in emergencies', in J. Crisp, C. Talbot and D. B. Cipollone (eds), *Learning for a Future: Refugee education in developing countries*. Geneva: UNHCR.

Sinclair, M. (2002), *Planning Education in and after Emergencies*. Paris: UNESCO International Institute for Educational Planning.

Slim, H. (1997), 'Doing the right thing: relief agencies, moral dilemmas and moral responsibility in political emergencies and war'. *Disasters 21*(3), 244–57.

Sommers, M. (2004), *Co-ordinating Education during Emergencies and Reconstruction: Challenges and responsibilities*. Paris: UNESCO International Institute for Educational Planning.

Steets, J., Grünewald, F., Binder, de Geoffroy, V., Kauffmann, D., Krüger, S., Meier, C. and Sokpoh, B. (2010), *Cluster Approach Evaluation 2. Synthesis Report*. IASC Cluster Approach Evaluation, 2nd Phase. Berlin: Plaisians.

Stoddard, A., Harmer, A., Haver, K., Salomons, D. and Wheeler, V. (2007), *Cluster Approach Evaluation. Final*. Geneva: OCHA Evaluation and Studies Section.

Tomlinson, K. and Benefield, P. (2005), *Education and Conflict: Research and research possibilities*. Slough, UK: National Foundation for Educational Research.

Unerman, J. and O'Dwyer, B. (2005), 'Theorising accountability for NGO advocacy'. *Accounting, Auditing & Accountability Journal 19*(3), 350.

UNESCO. (2010a) *The Central Role of Education in the Millennium Development Goals*. Paris: UNESCO, with UNICEF, the Government of Qatar and Save the Children International.

UNESCO. (2010b), *Protecting Education from Attack: A state-of-the-art review*. Paris: UNESCO.

UNESCO. (2011), *Education for All Global Monitoring Report. The Hidden Crisis: Armed conflict and education*. Paris: UNESCO.

UNICEF/UNESCO. (2007), *A Human Rights-Based Approach to Education: A framework for the realization of children's right to education and rights within education*. New York: UNICEF/UNESCO.

UN Humanitarian Reform Support Unit. (HRSU) (2008), *Cluster Approach*. Retrieved 15 July 2011 from http://www.humanitarianreform.org/humanitarianreform/Default.aspx?tabid=70.

UN/IASC. (2006), *Real-time Evaluation. Cluster Approach – Pakistan Earthquake. Final Draft. Application of the IASC Cluster Approach in the South Asia Earthquake*. Retrieved 31 July 2011 from http://www.alnap.org/pool/files/818.pdf.

Vaux, T. (2006), 'Humanitarian trends and dilemmas'. *Development in Practice 16*(3), 240–54.

Wilensky, H. L. (1964), 'The professionalization of everyone?' *The American Journal of Sociology 70*(2), 137–58.

Global Aid Frameworks: Application of *INEE Minimum Standards* for Advocacy, Coordination and Quality Education Provision for Burmese Refugees in Thailand

2

Fred Ligon, Tzvetomira Laub and Allison Anderson

Chapter Outline

Introduction   33

Case study   37

    Applying *INEE Minimum Standards* on the
      Thailand–Burma border   38
    Responding to an acute emergency in a chronic crisis   41

Conclusion   46

Introduction
Zuki Karpinska

The MDGs, especially 2 and 3 and the Dakar Framework for Action's EFA targets are arguably the principal global frameworks for aid agencies concerned with education (see Chapter 1). Yet, neither the MDGs nor the EFA goals offer any guidance on how the targets can be achieved. These frameworks provide the end-points of developing-country government and external aid efforts, but not the blueprints.

The creation of the humanitarian aid field's foremost attempt to provide guidance specifically to those responsible for disaster assistance, the *Sphere Humanitarian Charter and Minimum Standards in Humanitarian Response* (*Sphere Standards*: Sphere Project, 2011; now on its third edition), followed the catastrophic failure that was 1994 Rwanda and its aftermath. The number of aid institutions that mushroomed along the eastern border of then-Zaire swelled exponentially in response to the influx of refugees and available aid funding; sadly, many casualties resulted from 'the incompetence of the relief operation' (Vaux, 2006: 247). Formed in 1997 by NGOs and the Red Cross/Red Crescent, the Sphere Project provides an operational framework for the planning and implementation of aid (Sphere Project, 2011). The resultant *Sphere Standards* address five humanitarian aid sectors – water supply and sanitation, nutrition, food aid, shelter and health services – but not education.

As a response to the omission of education from the Sphere handbook, thirty-one high-level education practitioners from a variety of international NGOs and UN agencies met in Paris in 2002 for an 'experts' workshop' to discuss the possibility of establishing standards. This meeting resulted from a desire to ensure the highest standards for emergency response in the education sector, and the marginalization of education as a humanitarian response through, for example, the Sphere process (INEE, 2002). A then-negligible in number INEE network approached the management committee of the Sphere Project, but were denied their request to include education in the Sphere handbook. The purpose of the 2002 Paris meeting was to 'determine the feasibility of developing and implementing a set of standards for education in emergencies' (INEE, 2002: 3). If it was decided at the meeting that standardization of practice was needed for EiE practitioners and policy-makers, those attending were to agree on a process for developing such standards. The group unanimously decided to move ahead with the standard-setting enterprise and to adopt the development framework used by Sphere, so that an education chapter could easily be added to the Sphere handbook if such a decision were to be made in the future (INEE, 2002).

The resultant handbook was the 2004 edition of the Inter-Agency Network for Education in Emergencies (INEE) *Minimum Standards for Education in Emergencies, Chronic Crises and Early Reconstruction* (*INEE Minimum Standards*) (see Chapter 1), developed after a two-year process of consultation involving 2,250 participants from over 50 countries (INEE, 2004). Arguably, the handbook represents the first inter-agency, comprehensive attempt to codify (i.e. make explicit) the tacit (i.e. implicit) knowledge held by EiE professionals: a documentation of the experiences of the many individuals concerned with EiE provision. Unlike the MDG and EFA targets but similar to the *Sphere*

Standards, this global framework provides guidance on implementation of the standards established. Importantly, unlike the three other above-mentioned frameworks, the INEE framework provides no numerical targets.

The product of this global standard-setting enterprise, the *INEE Minimum Standards* handbook, was consensually produced. Consensus may be defined as exploring 'various conflicting viewpoints and possibilities, focusing them, and directing them towards an entente that all acknowledge' (Moscovici & Doise, 1994: 1). Participation of a range of stakeholders – from teachers to policy-makers – was essential to this process of consensus-building, so that the resulting guidance would benefit from wide recognition, and thus legitimacy.

Consensus-building, in this instance, required the development of 'universal' guidance: that which could be applicable to all settings. In the 2004 edition of the *INEE Minimum Standards*, for instance, access and learning environment standard 3 on facilities states: '[e]ducation facilities are conducive to the physical well-being of learners'; a key indicator specifies: '[c]lass space and seating arrangements [should be] in line with an agreed ratio of space per learner and teacher'; and the relevant 'guidance note' states: 'a locally realistic standard should be set for maximum class size' (INEE, 2004: 47). The consensually produced guidance for classroom size, therefore, does not provide a numerical maximum. This is the case for all of the key indicators (2004 edition) and key actions (2010 edition) compiled in the *INEE Minimum Standards*. Rather, the guidance within the handbook is designed to be 'contextualized', which refers to the process of adapting a tool, document or policy to a specific context, rendering them relevant to local experience and the given environment, in terms of geographical, sociocultural, economic and political factors.

According to INEE, the handbook was developed in order to enhance the quality of educational preparedness, response and recovery; increase access to safe and relevant learning opportunities; and ensure accountability in providing these services. The guidance in the *INEE Minimum Standards* handbook is designed for use in a range of situations, including disasters caused by natural hazards and conflict, in both protracted and rapid-onset situations a and emergencies in rural and urban environments.[1] The focus is on ensuring quality, coordinated humanitarian response: meeting the educational rights and needs of people affected by disaster through processes that assert their dignity. The handbook aims to provide guidance on how to prepare for and respond to acute emergencies in ways that reduce risk, improve future preparedness and lay a solid foundation for quality education. The guidance is intended to contribute to building stronger, sustainable education systems in the recovery and development stages following a crisis.

Since its launch in 2004, the *INEE Minimum Standards* handbook has been used in over eighty countries to promote quality education in emergencies through to recovery. In evaluations of the handbook (see Women's Commission, 2006; Karpinska, 2007, 2008) users have related that it provides a common framework and facilitates the development of shared objectives among different stakeholders, including members of governments, communities and international agencies.

The *INEE Minimum Standards* define the goals for access to quality education in universal terms, while the 2004 edition's key indicators and the 2010 edition's key actions present the specific steps that are required to achieve each standard (see Box 2.1 for an overview of the content). Since every context is different, the key indicators/key actions in the handbook must be adapted to each local situation. Context, including available resources, and the stage of the emergency must be considered in determining locally relevant actions as put forward in the handbook. The process of contextualization ideally should occur prior to the onset of any emergency as part of educational contingency planning and preparedness. Experience has shown that contextualization is more effective when carried out as a participatory and collaborative exercise.

Box 2.1 Original version of the *INEE Minimum Standards*

In the 2004 *INEE Minimum Standards for Education in Emergencies, Chronic Crises, and Early Reconstruction,* standards, accompanying indicators and guidance notes are represented in five categories:[2]

- *Minimum Standards Common to All Categories*: focuses on the essential areas of community participation and utilizing local resources when applying the standards in this handbook, as well as ensuring that emergency education responses are based on an initial assessment that is followed by an appropriate response and continued monitoring and evaluation.
- *Access and Learning Environment*: focuses on partnerships to promote access to learning opportunities as well as inter-sectoral linkages with, for example, health, water and sanitation, food aid (nutrition) and shelter, to enhance security and physical, cognitive and psychological well-being.
- *Teaching and Learning*: focuses on critical elements that promote effective teaching and learning: (1) curriculum, (2) training, (3) instruction and (4) assessment.
- *Teachers and Other Education Personnel*: focuses on the administration and management of human resources in the field of education, including recruitment and selection, conditions of service and supervision and support.
- *Education Policy and Coordination*: focuses on policy formulation and enactment, planning and implementation and coordination.

This chapter presents a case study of the application of *INEE Minimum Standards* by the US NGO World Education to strengthen education programming in response to the needs of refugees from Burma, displaced along the Thailand–Burma border. The case study describes the process and lessons learned in the adaptation and usage of the *INEE Minimum Standards* in the context of a chronic crisis situation, in which camp-based displacement is further exacerbated by periodic new displacement.

Case study
Fred Ligon, Tzvetomira Laub and Allison Anderson

Background

For decades, Burma has seen active ethnic minority resistance to its military government. The Karen National Union (KNU), one of the largest ethnic resistance groups, was increasingly pushed toward the Thailand border where periodic dry season offensives by the Burmese military forced ethnic minorities to temporarily seek refuge on the Thai side of the border. In 1984, the Burmese military launched a major offensive, which broke through the KNU front lines opposite Thailand's Tak Province resulting in 10,000 refugees fleeing across the border. With the Burmese military maintaining their position, and not withdrawing as they would usually do during the rainy season, many refugees were forced to remain in Thailand.

In 1984, the Burmese military had launched annual dry season offensives, taken control of new territory and established new bases; these actions increased the refugee population in Thailand to approximately 80,000. Further, following the 1988 democracy movement, the Mon and Karenni ethnic group areas were militarized, leading to a further refugee influx into Thailand. The 1995 fall of Manerplaw – a major KNU stronghold – and years of forced village relocations and human rights abuses since 1996 have also added to the number of refugees. As of 2010, nine camps on the Thailand–Burma border house more than 140,000 refugees, with new arrivals every month. The position of the Thai government is that the population arriving from Burma to Thailand are displaced persons, rather than refugees, who live in temporary shelters rather than refugee camps. Importantly, Thailand is not a signatory to the 1951 Convention Relating to the Status of Refugees.

The Committee for Coordination of Services to Displaced Persons in Thailand (CCSDPT), a network of NGOs authorized by the Thai Ministry of Interior to work with the displaced population, provides support for basic services in the camps – health, food security and nutrition, shelter, water and sanitation and education. Unlike other refugee contexts where the United Nations High Commission for Refugees (UNHCR) coordinates the service delivery, Thai authorities secure the camps but the refugees have a major role in camp management, largely through camp committees, refugee-led departments and community-based organizations.

Founded in 1951 to meet the needs of the educationally disadvantaged, World Education has worked in over fifty countries. World Education's mission in Thailand is to provide safe access to quality education for refugees and migrants. For the most part this is accomplished by working to build the capacity of refugees and migrants to manage their own education programmes and activities. Since 1999, World Education – a member of the CCSDPT – has implemented and supported programme activities in pre-service teacher training, curriculum development, school management training, adult literacy, special needs education, English immersion programming and other post-secondary courses along the Thailand–Burma border.

Applying *INEE Minimum Standards* on the Thailand–Burma border

World Education's involvement in the provision of refugee assistance in the context of the chronic crisis on the Thailand–Burma border provided the motivation to participate actively in the development of the *INEE Minimum Standards* in 2003–2004 and to join the INEE Working Group on Minimum Standards, tasked with development of the handbook and its promotion worldwide. World Education together with ZOA Refugee Care held three consultations in 2003. Representatives of NGOs and community-based organizations participated in two of these consultations while Burmese refugee education leaders participated in the third (see Box 2.2). Subsequent to the launch of the handbook in December 2004, World Education conducted orientations, training sessions and presentations on *INEE Minimum Standards* at various fora.

Box 2.2 *INEE Minimum Standards* – Incorporating the Refugee Voice

On 5 April 2004, thirty-five refugee education leaders gathered in World Education's bamboo and thatch training room near the entrance to the Mae La Refugee Camp, a one-hour drive outside the border town of Mae Sot. The refugee education leaders were developing standards and indicators based on their context, which would feed into the larger global process to develop minimum standards for education. This was their first introduction to INEE and, for many of them, their first experience with identifying and developing standards and indicators. The concepts of *minimum* and *standard* were explained and then for three and a half hours they worked in groups to draft standards and indicators for 'teaching and learning' and 'teachers and other education personnel' domains. The consultation facilitator reviewed the work of each group as he walked around the room; periodically he asked for their attention to reiterate the concept of *minimum*. To the facilitator, many of the standards and indicators that the refugees were drafting appeared to be set too high – perhaps more aspirational than practical when defining an emergency response. It was during one of these pauses for clarification that a refugee education leader, a highly respected woman in their community, stood up to give voice to a powerful observation.

We understand the difference between standards and indicators. We understand the meaning of minimum. And, we know we are just refugees. But, why should we accept less for our children than you want for yours?

Indeed. Education is a right: a fundamental right and one that must be reflected in quality standards.

In 2005, the World Education Country Director deemed it impractical to introduce the handbook as a framework to totally redesign the education programme, which World Education had been implementing for five years. The Country Director determined that a more useful form of application of the *INEE Minimum Standards* would be to use them in monitoring and evaluation. To this end, the Director developed the Internal Reflection Tool based on the experience of contextualization of the handbook in Afghanistan (see Box 2.3).[3]

Box 2.3 International Reflection Tool

Standard Category: Access and Learning Environment
Standard 1: Equal Access – All individuals have access to quality and relevant education opportunities.

Terms and Definitions	Practice in Thailand	Verification	Key Indicators Noted	Comment
Access: camp residents are able to enrol and participate in education offered in the camps.	There is now a much greater range of education opportunities offered in the refugee camps then at the onset of the emergency, but the ability to do this is impacted by funding.	Karen Education Department/Karenni Education Department responses to questions posed by UNHCR and UNICEF about access.	No individual is denied access to education and learning opportunities because of discrimination.	Married and/or pregnant youth are not allowed to study. CCSDPT Education Subcommittee intervened but there has been no change in policy.
Quality: attainment of a level of excellence meeting accepted standards (local or international).	Access still remains an issue for some, such as youth who get married while they are still students or who get pregnant.	CCSDPT annual proposals [and Director Reports from ZOA and JRS.	A range of formal and non-formal education opportunities is progressively provided.	Since the onset of the emergency, yes.
Relevant: a range of education choices are available (primary, secondary, higher education, life skills, vocational training, non-formal, literacy, accelerated learning, etc.) so that education offered is appropriate to individual learners.	The Thai Ministry of Education (MOE) has increased its involvement in the refugee camps in the last 3 years through provision of Thai language classes and efforts to create quality standardized curricula in the refugee camp schools. There is hope that this could lead eventually to accreditation or some other form of validation of learning such as taking an examination, which would allow for a certificate recognized by Thailand. World Education is not involved directly with this effort but works on a parallel initiative with MOE in migrant education.	Organizational experience. CCSDPT Director Meetings Reports from ZOA and WE's Deputy Director.	Through training and sensitization, communities become increasingly involved in ensuring the rights of all members to a quality and relevant education. Sufficient resources are made available by authorities, donors, NGOs and other partners to ensure continuity and quality. The education program is recognized by the education authorities of the host country and/or country of origin.	Special education: awareness raising has only been partially effective, particularly with the camp educational leaders. Reproductive Health: there's still resistance to introducing this. Funding by donors has not been consistent or sufficient. There are still unaddressed gaps in services. In progress: this will primarily involve ZOA and MOE and be dependent upon production of a quality, standard curriculum. Follow-up: ask for regular updates at the monthly CCSDPT Education Subcommittee meetings.

The Internal Reflection Tool provided an opportunity to look at the *INEE Minimum Standards* and elaborate on how each applies to the reality of the Thailand–Burma border. The key indicators that accompany each standard in the 2004 edition were reviewed to determine the extent to which the standard was being achieved as well as to generate ideas for actions that could be taken to reach the standard.

In 2009, using the Internal Reflection Tool, World Education conducted an audit of its role in education on the Thailand–Burma border. Subsequently, and in accordance with the development of the education sector of a CCSDPT-UNHCR five-year Strategic Framework, CCSDPT education organizations decided to add an intervention requiring all organizations to 'apply the *INEE Minimum Standards* in camp education programs' (CCSDPT-UNHCR Five-Year Strategic Framework for Durable Solutions: 11).

To further this commitment, the CCSDPT began conducting an expanded audit of the overall education response on the border in 2010. Such audits were to be conducted annually in the future. The Karen Refugee Committee Education Entity, a refugee-led organization that manages education in seven of the nine refugee camps, participated in the audit and will follow up on the audit's findings and recommendations.

In the same year, the Burmese Migrant Workers Education Committee (BMWEC), a network committee representing and supporting up to fifty migrant schools in the Mae Sot area, decided to pilot the Internal Reflection Tool in migrant schools within their network. In support of this, migrant school directors participated in a one-day training, facilitated by World Education, which provided an orientation on the *INEE Minimum Standards* handbook as well as introduced the directors to the Internal Reflection Tool, showing how to use it to monitor what was happening in their own schools. It was planned that the group of school directors would reassemble to share their findings at a later time and also participate in a follow-up training. If participants in this pilot determined that the use of the Tool helped them identify and address gaps in education provision at schools, the pilot project would be expanded to other schools in subsequent years.

Responding to an acute emergency in a chronic crisis

Although World Education and other organizations have focused for years on the response to the protracted refugee situation, an influx of new refugees in June 2009 highlighted the need for organizations to continually prepare to respond to an acute and unexpected emergency. Following several days of heavy shelling and fighting between armed groups in Burma's Karen State, more than 4,000 people, mostly women and children from the IDP camp Ler Per Her, crossed the border and settled in four locations north of Tha Song Yang District, north of the Mae La Refugee Camps.

Most new refugees wanted to stay close to the border to facilitate their return home once this was feasible, and chose to not seek shelter in one of the nearby refugee camps. Had the refugees wanted the protection offered by being in a camp, camp organizations would have been well prepared to provide a coordinated response to their arrival as systems and procedures were in place. However, the influx of many refugees who wanted to stay outside the camps complicated the response. Which organization should be the lead agency? What resources were available? What communication mechanisms needed to be in place? Which organizations should be invited to coordination meetings? The following account will provide observations and lessons learned based on the experience of the education sector.

Although some of the education NGOs within CCSDPT were part of the initial humanitarian response, obtaining permission for the education sector to be represented at coordination meetings with UNHCR and the Thai government and military was not easy to facilitate. It was clear that the Thai authorities did not want the refugees to stay in Thailand; the provision of education services might have implied permanence to the settlement of the refugees within Thai borders in a way that provision of food or health services did not.

In preparation for an education sector meeting, World Education adapted the situational analysis and needs assessment tools from the *INEE Minimum Standards* handbook (INEE, 2004: 30–8), and shared them with the education NGOs planning the coordinated education response. These tools were adapted for use in the local context. Adaptation primarily entailed streamlining, or removing text from the guidance that did not pertain to the needs of refugees from Burma, resulting in a shorter and easier to use tool. Those involved in the streamlining, or contextualization, process observed that some of the information to be gleaned from questions proposed in the handbook might not need to be requested, given the nature of this particular emergency. Two CCSDPT organizations – Adventist Development and Relief Agency (ADRA) and Shanti Volunteer Association (SVA) – which were in a position to conduct site visits, made further adaptations before using the tools in the field.

World Education, which chairs the CCSDPT Education Subcommittee, secured a meeting with Thai authorities to discuss provision of education services in August 2009. World Education requested that the education sector be represented at future sector-coordination meetings, but Thai authorities did not approve the request. As mentioned above, for the Thai authorities, the provision of education foretold a possibly more permanent settlement of these refugees from Burma. Nevertheless, the meeting allowed a useful discussion on international standards, the protection that education can offer to children and the importance of child-friendly, safe learning spaces. Thai authorities expressed a concern that NGOs might try to encourage the refugees to stay in Thailand to complete their education, thus creating an attractive learning environment that could draw in more refugees. Ultimately and as agreed at that meeting, the World Education Director, as Chair of the CCSDPT Education Subcommittee, drafted a Letter of Understanding addressing these points. Although an invitation to be part of a multi-sector coordination effort would have been preferable as this would have strengthened links with other sectors involved in emergency response, this dialogue with the Thai authorities, with the *INEE Minimum Standards* framing the discussion to advocate for access to education, resulted in agreement to a measure of education support.

Subsequently, CCSDPT and other NGOs met in Mae Sot to map out available resources, funding and staff. Organizations that could provide immediate support were identified as well as organizations that could provide mid-term or long-term support if needed. ADRA had access to emergency funds that were immediately available so ADRA was identified as the lead agency with supportive roles identified for other organizations.

Some of the refugees displaced in Tha Song Yang district returned to Burma, amidst concerns about the voluntary nature of their return and about their ability to return safely due to continuing armed conflict and land mines. The protracted refugee situation on the Thailand–Burma border shows no signs of abating. CCSDPT member organizations will continue to respond to the refugee situation while working to develop contingency coordination plans to be better prepared for another large influx of refugees.

World Education's introduction and contextualization of the *INEE Minimum Standards* and the CCSDPT response to the acute emergency amidst a chronic crisis illustrate good practices synthesized in the handbook. First, following the guidance in the handbook on community participation, World Education involved other NGOs, community-based organizations and – in the case of migrants – the school directors in monitoring schools and the provision of education services (see Box 2.4). Second, in accordance with the guidance in the Coordination standard, World Education – representing CCSDPT – engaged the Thai authorities in discussions and decision-making on the provision of education, recorded the reached agreement in a Letter of Understanding and contributed to the mobilization of resources from the CCSDPT members and others (see Box 2.4). And third, in accordance with the guidance in Education Policy Standard 1 on Law and Policy Formulation, the members of the CCSDPT Education Subcommittee worked with others in the education sector to develop a response plan outlining members' capacity for education response and setting up coordination structures (see Box 2.4).

Box 2.4 Selections from the 2004 edition of the *INEE Minimum Standards*, adapted[4] for use along the Thailand–Burma border

Community Participation Standard 1: Participation

Community members participate actively, transparently and without discrimination in analysis, planning, design, implementation, monitoring and evaluation of education responses.

Key indicators (to be read in conjunction with the guidance notes)

- A range of community members participate actively in prioritizing and planning education activities to ensure safe, effective and equitable delivery of education.
- Community education committees include representatives of all vulnerable groups.
- Children and youth participate actively in the development, implementation, monitoring and evaluation of education activities.
- A wide range of community members participate in assessments, context analyses, social audits of education activities, joint budget reviews and disaster risk reduction and conflict mitigation activities.
- Training and capacity building opportunities are available to community members.

Coordination Standard 1: Coordination

Coordination mechanisms for education are in place and support stakeholders working to ensure access to and continuity of quality education.

Key indicators (to be read in conjunction with the guidance notes)

- Education authorities, which are responsible for fulfilling the right to education, assume a leadership role for education response, including convening and participating in coordination mechanisms with other education stakeholders.
- An inter-agency coordination committee coordinates assessment, planning, information management, resource mobilization, capacity development and advocacy.
- A range of levels and types of education are considered in coordination activities.

- Education authorities, donors, UN agencies, NGOs, communities and other stakeholders use timely, transparent, equitable and coordinated financing structures to support education activities.
- Transparent mechanisms for sharing information on the planning and coordination of responses exist within the coordination committee and across coordination groups.
- Joint assessments are carried out to identify capacities and gaps in education response.
- All stakeholders adhere to the principles of equality, transparency, responsibility and accountability to achieve results.

Education Policy Standard 2: Planning and Implementation

Education activities take into account international and national educational policies, laws, standards and plans and the learning needs of affected populations.

Key indicators (to be read in conjunction with the guidance notes)

- Formal and non-formal education programmes reflect international and national legal frameworks and policies.
- Planning and implementation of educational activities are integrated with other emergency response sectors.
- Emergency education programmes are linked to national education plans and strategies and are integrated with longer-term development of the education sector.
- Education authorities develop and implement national and local education plans that prepare for and respond to future and current emergencies.
- Financial, technical, material and human resources are sufficient for effective and transparent development of education policy and for planning and implementation of education programmes.

The institutions involved in the application of the *INEE Minimum Standards* on the Thailand–Burma border considered the handbook to be a helpful monitoring and evaluation tool. Lessons learned include: to be effective, the *INEE Minimum Standards* need to be contextualized to reflect a given situation; the development of World Education's Internal Reflection Tool and its use in audits served that purpose. Locally identified and acceptable key indicators, or key actions, are crucial to effective use of the handbook. Whenever possible, contextualization of the *INEE Minimum Standards* should occur prior to the onset of an emergency.

Moreover, the *INEE Minimum Standards* do not need to drive a project or supplant existing standards. Rather, since the handbook defines access to quality education, they can coexist with and complement other measures and standards. And even if the national authorities are not aware of the existence of the *INEE Minimum Standards*, the handbook provides an entry point for NGO dialogue and advocacy with authorities.

Finally, the experience in Thailand indicates that the process of organizational learning and discovery is important, if not necessary, when embarking on a participatory, collaborative exercise with other stakeholders to provide education responses to the refugee situation. To this effect, refugees participated in the development of the *INEE Minimum Standards* through their participation in one of three consultations. World Education staff did not drastically change their work plans nor ways of implementing their work. Instead, World Education staff participated in training and orientations with the *Minimum Standards* being seen as a tool that could be useful in monitoring and improving their work. World Education and colleagues from other education NGOs were able to jointly recognize the value of the *INEE Minimum Standards* as the basis of a tool for monitoring and to institutionalize the handbook as a network document.

Subsequent to writing this account, there was another large influx of refugees along the border – up to 10,000 by some reports. Many of the refugees preferred to blend into Thai border communities due to fears that they might be sent home. In the midst of the protracted refugee situation on the Thailand–Burma border, both recent influxes created the need for an effective emergency education response; one that highlights access to education (in whatever form that is possible given the local context) and the protection education affords. Community participation and coordination are crucial for an effective response as a new crisis unfolds. The *INEE Minimum Standards*, the product of a global consensus, have been acknowledged by CCSDPT education NGOs as being the framework that informs emergency education response and a way of measuring how effective that response may be.

Conclusion
Zuki Karpinska

The 'embeddedness' of a guiding document or framework may be referred to as 'institutionalization', what used to be known as 'mainstreaming'.

> [The] process of ensuring an issue is placed within wider strategic and institutional processes is known as 'mainstreaming'. Mainstreaming is a comprehensive process, which ensures that an issue and approach is systematically addressed across all strategies, programmes and initiatives undertaken by any agency

for example EuropeAid) or process (for example a Poverty Reduction Strategy
Paper/Country Strategy Paper). Mainstreaming is based on an understanding that
a partial, isolated or piecemeal approach to the issue would be at best ineffective
and at worst counterproductive. (Sherrif, 2003: 6)

Institutionalization here refers to the ways in which a particular idea has
been integrated and formally incorporated into institutions' policies, procedures, operations, organizational culture, structures and systems, as well
as the priority that institutions place on this issue (Cummings & Worley,
2001) Institutionalization is the 'gold standard' to which the humanitarian
aid industry frameworks strive, meaning that at no point during the project
cycle – during conceptualization, planning, implementation, monitoring and
evaluation – will attention to the idea/issue/focus be omitted.

For instance, the MDG and EFA frameworks reflect the recognition of the
global 'education gap' that has resulted in privileging boys education over that
of girls in some contexts. Attention to 'gender', in the last two decades, may
be said to have become 'institutionalized' within the humanitarian aid industry. Almost all project proposals (i.e. the framework of a given intervention or
course of action) contain the words 'gender equality', 'women' or 'girls'. There
is also wide recognition on the part of aid agencies that girls' education is the
single best development investment, an argument posited by Summers in his
influential text *Investing in All the People* (Summers, 1992). The rationale for this
is that the cost–benefit ratio of educating girls is much greater than any other
form of development aid intervention, due to a roll-out effect that extends to
wider communities; for example, women who have completed primary school
are likely to have delayed marriage, have fewer and healthier children, enjoy
greater agricultural gains and educate their own children as a result. In some
circumstances – and often partially due to policies and practices that dispro-
portionately favour girl children – boys have, in fact, fallen behind in schooling
in certain subjects or grade levels. As 'gender considerations' in aid discourse
have long been synonymous with awareness of the marginalization of girls and
women, awareness of and attention to the particular needs of boys and young
men have not yet been institutionalized on the same level as those of girls.

A crucial goal for INEE is to 'institutionalize' the *INEE Minimum Standards*
handbook, aiming to establish it as a substantive – and utilized – framework
for EiE action. The guidance provided within the *INEE Minimum Standards*
must necessarily be contextualized in order to prove useful. The crisis-specific
process of contextualization of the handbook is strongly encouraged by the
INEE Secretariat. In the revised 2010 edition of the handbook, the necessity

for contextualization of the content is made far more explicit than in the 2004 edition.

The case study within this chapter provides two examples of the adaption, that is, contextualization, of the *INEE Minimum Standards* to a localized chronic crisis situation. The case study authors underscore that, ideally, such contextualization should have occurred prior to the onset of an emergency; in this case, however, the handbook had not yet existed when Burmese populations began to find refuge along the Thai border. The case study authors also indicate that, rather than revise programming already under way (i.e. embed the *INEE Minimum Standards* from the outset of project planning), the select guidance from the handbook was used to devise a monitoring framework. Finally, the authors highlight the need for wide participation in the adoption of the adapted (i.e. contextualized) guidance – from government authorities to school directors to community members to NGO representatives. The test for institutionalization of the *INEE Minimum Standards* will be whether future projects consult the handbook and contextualize its guidance in future programme planning – including project proposals, implementation plans and M&E frameworks – with or without the leadership of World Education, an organization strongly committed to the dissemination and use of the handbook.

The MDG and EFA goals are still far more institutionalized in humanitarian aid practice within the education sector than the *INEE Minimum Standards*. This is conceivably due to the earlier date of their development, to their brevity and – most importantly – to government commitments to achieve these goals. However, the handbook has gained great exposure with governments through the July 2010 adoption of the UN General Assembly resolution on 'The Right to Education in Emergency Situations (A/64/L.58)', in which the *INEE Minimum Standards* are named as a framework to improve educational provision in crisis contexts: a tremendous coup for the INEE network. To be 'universally' useful as a framework in all crises, however, contextualization is key.

Key questions

- How do those concerned with planning for education as a humanitarian response make sense of key global frameworks and targets?
- How do planners perceive the limitations of these frameworks and (do they) attempt to compensate for these limitations?

Notes

1   For more information on the *INEE Minimum Standards*, visit www.ineesite.org/standards.

2   Copied verbatim from INEE (2008), *Talking Points: Education in Emergencies, INEE and the INEE Minimum Standards*, revised November 2008. Retrieved 31 July 2011 from http://ineesite.org//uploads/documents/store/MSEE_talking_points.pdf.

3   The efforts of Partnership for Advancing Community-Based Education (PACE-A) in Afghanistan (see Chapter 6) to contextualize the *INEE Minimum Standards* informed the development of the Internal Reflection Tool in Thailand.

4   Vetted tools to support the implementation, adaptation and usage of the *INEE Minimum Standards* can be found in the *INEE Toolkit* online at toolkit.ineesite.org.

Further reading

INEE. (2010), *Minimum Standards for Education: Preparedness, response, recovery*. Retrieved 31 July 2011 from http://www.ineesite.org/uploads/documents/store/Minimum_Standards_2010_eng.pdf. The revised edition of the essential guide for education provision in emergencies: the documentation of the experiences of thousands of individuals worldwide concerned with EiE provision.

Bromley, P. and Andina, M. (2010), 'Standardizing chaos: a neo-institutional analysis of the INEE Minimum Standards for Education in Emergencies, Chronic crises and Early Reconstruction', *Compare: A Journal of Comparative and International Education 40*(5), 575–88. A scholarly look at the emergence of EiE provision as a professional field through an examination of the development of the *INEE Minimum Standards* and the implications of the handbook's existence.

References

Bromley, P. and Andina, M. (2010), 'Standardizing chaos: a neo-institutional analysis of the INEE Minimum Standards for Education in Emergencies, Chronic Crises and Early Reconstruction', *Compare: A Journal of Comparative and International Education 40*(5), 575–88.

Cummings, T. G. and Worley, C. G. (2001), *Organizational Development and Change*, 7th edn. Cincinnati, OH: South-Western.

INEE. (2004), *Minimum Standards for Education in Emergencies, Chronic Crises and Early Reconstruction*. Retrieved 31 July 2011 from http://www.ineesite.org/minimum_standards/MSEE_report.pdf.

INEE. (2008), *Talking Points: Education in emergencies, INEE and the INEE Minimum Standards*, revised November 2008. Retrieved 31 July 2011 from http://ineesite.org//uploads/documents/store/MSEE_talking_points.pdf.

INEE. (2010), *Minimum Standards for Education: Preparedness, response, recovery*. Retrieved 31 July 2011 from http://www.ineesite.org/uploads/documents/store/Minimum_Standards_2010_eng.pdf.

Karpinska, Z. (2007), *An Evaluation of the INEE Minimum Standards for Education in Emergencies, Chronic Crises and Early Reconstruction: A Pakistan case study*. Retrieved 31 July 2011 from http://ineesite.org/uploads/documents/store/doc_1_INEE_MS_Pakistan_Case_Study1pdf.

Karpinska, Z. (2008), *An Evaluation of the INEE Minimum Standards for Education in Emergencies, Chronic Crises and Early Reconstruction: A Uganda case study*. Retrieved 31 July 2011 from http://www.ineesite.org/uploads/documents/store/Final_Uganda_Report.pdf.

Moscovici, S. and Doise, W. (1994), *Conflict and Consensus: A general theory of collective decisions*. Translated by W. D. Halls. London: Sage.

Sherrif, A. (2003), *Mainstreaming SALW, Landmine and ERW Issues in Development and Humanitarian Processes and Institutions*. United Nations Institute for Disarmament Research.

Sphere Project. (2011), *The Sphere Project Humanitarian Charter and Minimum Standards in Humanitarian Response*. The Sphere Project. Retrieved 31 July 2011 from http://www.sphereproject.org/content/view/720/200/lang,english/.

Summers, L. H. (1992), *Investing in All the People*. World Bank Working Paper Series 905. Washington, DC: World Bank.

Vaux, T. (2006), 'Humanitarian trends and dilemmas'. *Development in Practice 16*(3), 240–54.

Women's Commission for Refugee Women and Children (2006), Inter-Agency Network for Education in Emergencies Minimum Standards for Education in Emergencies, Chronic Crises and Early Reconstruction: Darfur Case Study. New York: Women's Commission for Refugee Women and Children. Retrieved 31 July 2011 from http://www.ineesite.org/uploads/documents/store/INEE_MS_WRC_Darfur_Case_Study.pdf.

Donor Policies: The Evolution and Development of DFID's Commitment to Education in Fragile States (2000–10)

3

Peter Colenso

Chapter Outline

Introduction   51
Case study   52
    Fragile States   52
    Education in fragile states   54
    Patterns of UK investment   56
Why did DFID decide to scale-up support to education
    in fragile states?   58
Conclusion   65

Introduction
Zuki Karpinska

The premise of this volume does not belie Escobar's (1992) observation that 'the concept of planning embodies the belief that social change can be engineered and directed, produced at will' (p. 132). On some level, each of the institutions and decision-makers highlighted in this collection of case studies relies on a particular theory of change, a belief that – given strategic input, training, behaviour modification, technology and/or funding – a specific population in a specific context will have a greater chance of claiming their universal rights. Often, for this change to occur at the individual level, the larger socioeconomic and political context will also have to change. These theories of change within the humanitarian aid industry may be considered discursive trends, conceptual frameworks for interpreting and analysing the development and humanitarian aid environment.

One such recent discursive trend has been that of state fragility, a concept with no globally agreed-upon definition and, therefore, no agreed-upon list of fragile states.

> Concern for state fragility covers a broad spectrum, embracing claims that fragile states present direct threats to Western national security, alongside arguments that dysfunctional state institutions are the key obstacle to sustainable development. The debate thus links security and development communities in a vague, yet firm, claim that addressing state fragility is one of the most pressing policy questions of our time. (Andersen, 2008: 7)

This discursive trend has been gaining traction, as evidenced by the steady emergence of fragile states policies among the donor community, and the establishment of a dedicated Working Group on Education and Fragility within INEE, the global, professional network for those concerned with education provision in crisis situations.

The case study in this chapter outlines the processes leading to the commitment of UK's DFID to humanitarian and development aid support to fragile states. The study describes the emergence of the 'fragile states' discourse as well as that on education and fragility, and tracks DFID's interest in and funding for education in fragile states. The study also speculates as to why this policy decision was made.

Case study
Peter Colenso

Fragile states

In the last decade, development agencies have become increasingly concerned with the impact of weak and ineffective states. The UK government is no exception. Indeed, DFID has arguably steered its policy and resources towards fragile states to a greater degree than any other bilateral development agency. A range of factors have contributed to DFID's increasing focus on fragile and conflict-affected states; principle among which are: (i) a recognition that the MDGs will not be achieved without dramatic progress in fragile states and (ii) post-9/11, an increased focus on the costs of state fragility for all nations, both developing and donor countries.

Among donor agencies, definitions of, and institutional policy towards, fragile states variously emphasized 'state fragility' (e.g. USAID, DFID), 'poor performance' (e.g. World Bank, Asian Development Bank, UNDP, AusAID) and 'difficult partnerships' (e.g. OECD/DAC, European Commission) before coalescing around the term 'fragile states' (Moreno Torres & Anderson, 2004). A host of development agencies published policy positions on the concept of fragile states at approximately the same time, indicating a rising interest in the concept of fragility in the first few years of the new millennium.

In the early generation of analytical work on the subject, Branchflower et al. (2004) associated fragile states with the following characteristics: state collapse, loss of territorial control, low administrative capacity, political instability, neo-patrimonial politics, conflict and regressive polities. The DAC of the OECD provided a fourfold typology of fragile states: (i) deterioration, (ii) arrested development, (iii) post-conflict transition and (iv) early recovery. DFID's (2005) policy paper defined fragile states as 'states that cannot or will not deliver core functions to the majority of its people, particularly the poor'. It was this 2005 policy paper that provided an analytical and policy framework for increased UK support to fragile states, albeit an increase that was already underway, as is demonstrated below.

It is also important to note, however, that the concept of fragile states had, and has, its detractors. Some have rejected the distinction between fragile states and better performing states as inaccurate or unhelpful. Reasons cited include the following: measures of fragility are subjective (e.g. the World Bank's Country Policy and Institutional Assessment (CPIA) ratings); fragility is dynamic – states move into and out of fragility; 'good performers' may have pockets of fragility and even conflict (e.g. northern Uganda); a state-centric definition gives undue emphasis to the role of the state; fragility might be better analysed on a regional rather than state basis (e.g. West Africa, the Great Lakes region and the Caucasus); and/or defining 'fragility' as a lack of will to address poverty reduction defines fragility on donors' terms. Others have found the term frankly stigmatizing:

> We heard the terminology around 'fragile states'. We wish to underline the importance of being cautious in using this term. It is labelling countries in a

negative way, where we are trying to develop and become stronger and prouder nations.[1]

Yet, the concept of fragile states has certainly had, and continues to have, considerable traction (see, e.g., World Bank, 2011), particularly among donor agencies. DFID and others have argued that the concept has a high degree of analytical, policy and operational utility. This is a belief I share. Categorizing states in terms of fragility can highlight a common set of conditions (e.g. instability, weak institutions and/or very low capacity) that constrain development, which the conventional 'aid effectiveness' paradigm is less able to handle. So how has the concept and operationalization of fragile states played out in social sectors, including in education?

Education in fragile states

The emergence in the mid-2000s of the concept of 'fragile states' coincided with a renewed analytical focus on 'service delivery', positioned centre-stage in the development agenda by the World Bank's 2004 World Development Report *Making Services Work for the Poor* (World Bank, 2004). It is interesting for the purposes of this publication that the last few years are sandwiched between the analytical bookends of service delivery (World Bank, 2004) and fragile states (World Bank, 2011).

Bringing these two priorities together, a body of literature – influential to DFID, and some of it indeed commissioned by DFID – began to emerge on service delivery in fragile states (see e.g. Berry et al., 2004; Carlson et al., 2005; Laurence & Poole, 2005; Slaymaker et al., 2005), and on aid effectiveness in fragile states (see e.g. Leader & Colenso, 2005; ODI, 2005; Piciotto, 2005). The OECD/DAC began a 'Learning and Advisory Process' dedicated to service delivery in fragile states, culminating in the publication of *Principles of Good International Engagement in Fragile States* (OECD/DAC, 2005), subsequently updated. This body of analytical work, and emerging policy and operational guidance, was strongly shaped by DFID.

In parallel, a literature started emerging specifically on education and fragile states. In the literature review for my doctoral thesis, I grouped into three types and stages the literature on education and fragile states that emerged from the 1990s:

1. *Education in emergencies and in conflict* (late 1990s on): focusing on the impact of complex emergencies and conflict on education, the provision of education in these circumstances and the reconstruction of education systems and communities post-conflict;
2. *Analysis linking education and conflict* (2000 on): proposing a more subtle two-way understanding of the relationship between education and social unrest/conflict; drawing on broader conflict analysis to show how education might be a part of the problem as well as the solution;
3. *Aid effectiveness and service delivery in fragile states* (2002 on, but particularly 2004/2005): focusing on state fragility and institutional weaknesses as the key long-term development challenges; recognizing that aid that must support both the delivery of core services and the building of long-term institutional capacity (Colenso, 2005).

It is worth noting that this literature emerged principally from development agencies themselves – as opposed to academic literature – to service a growing policy and operational agenda.[2]

In parallel, development agencies had been working together to find joint policy and operational approaches, as well as programming guidance, including: INEE (see e.g. INEE, 2004); the World Bank (World Bank, 2005); the OECD DAC (see e.g. Rose & Greeley, 2006), and the EFA-FTI Fragile States Task Team (FTI Secretariat, 2007). Some agencies backed these new policy commitments with financial resources. In December 2006, the Netherlands pledged $201 million over four years to UNICEF to provide education services for children in conflict-affected states. NGOs also started campaigning for attention to education in fragile and conflict-affected states, most notably the Save the Children Fund, which launched its *Rewrite the Future* Campaign in 2006 (Save the Children, 2006).

The United Kingdom was at the forefront of this work, through former UK prime minister Gordon Brown's personal leadership on an issue close to his heart (e.g. hosting the May 2007 education conference in Brussels), and through Hilary Benn's leadership as then-Secretary of State for International Development (e.g. DFID's (2007) *Education beyond Borders* commitment[3]). Contrary to some sectors – such as HIV/AIDS – external pressure was not a strong driver for increased DFID/UK investment in fragile states. There was, however, some parliamentary interest. When then-Secretary of State for International Development Hilary Benn was asked in Parliament to explain his department's policy on education in fragile states, he replied in the following terms:

In the 2006 White Paper, DFID committed to providing greater support to those fragile states furthest behind on the Millennium Development Goals. The

UK will provide £8.5 billion over the next ten years to support education and this will include support for fragile states. In some fragile states, we will work through United Nations agencies and civil society where they can make better progress than governments in improving education. But we will also work to strengthen government systems to deliver services, where they are demonstrating a clear commitment to improve education but lack the resources and capacity to deliver.[4]

The next section discusses whether the UK commitment to fragile states, and to education in fragile states, was backed by resources. In short, it was.

Patterns of UK investment

This section looks at publicly available data to examine whether and how DFID increased its investments in fragile states – and specifically its investments in education – over a nine-year period from 2001.[5] I have chosen expenditure data as a unit of analysis for two reasons: (i) as a good proxy for political and institutional commitment and (ii) as a simple and transparent metric to track.

It should be noted that data used in this section track only DFID's bilateral aid to education, and not aid channelled through multilateral organizations such as the World Bank and the European Commission; it therefore under-represents DFID funding for education in fragile states. However, it does serve as a good proxy of DFID institutional commitment, as bilateral funding is allocated by DFID alone whereas multilateral aid is allocated on the basis of shareholder, board member and institutional interest.

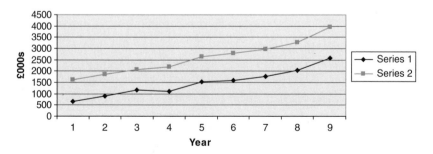

Figure 3.1 UK bilateral aid 2001–09 (total and fragile states)

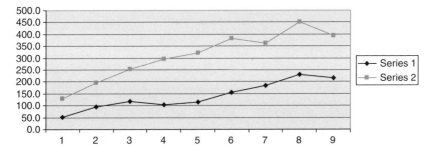

Figure 3.2 UK bilateral aid to Education 2001–09 (total and fragile states)

Figure 3.1 shows UK bilateral aid for the period 2001–09: total aid and – within that – bilateral aid to fragile states.[6] Total bilateral aid rose from £1.6 billion in 2001 to £3.9 billion in 2009; over the same period, bilateral aid to fragile states rose from £0.6 billion to £2.6 billion. The share of the total bilateral programme going to fragile states thus rose from 41 per cent of the portfolio to almost 65 per cent. The data therefore shows that UK bilateral aid to fragile states rose substantially over the first decade of the new millennium, in both absolute terms and as a proportion of DFID's overall bilateral expenditure.

So would we observe the same pattern if we look within UK bilateral aid specifically to the education sector? Figure 3.2 shows UK bilateral aid to education for the period 2001–09: total aid to education and – within that – bilateral aid to education in fragile states. Total bilateral aid to education rose from £128 million in 2001 to £395 million in 2009; over the same period, bilateral aid to education in fragile states rose from £51 million to £215 million. The share of the total bilateral education programme going to fragile states thus rose from 40 per cent of the portfolio to 54 per cent. While the 14 per cent rise in the share of the portfolio for education is less than the 24 per cent rise observed in the total bilateral programme (Figure 3.1), this still arguably represents a substantial increase in funding for education in fragile states, in both absolute and proportionate terms.[7]

Where did the bulk of this education spending take place? Figure 3.3 shows the nine countries where cumulative expenditure exceeded 100 million over this period. Of the countries listed, four are fragile states: Afghanistan, Bangladesh, Ethiopia and Kenya. The influence of Ethiopia on patterns of

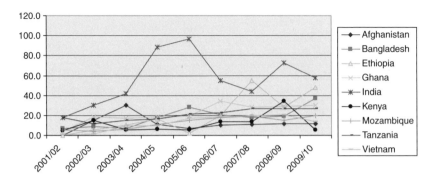

Figure 3.3 UK bilateral aid to Education 2001–09 (nine recipient countries where cumulative expenditure exceeded £100m)

overall expenditure in fragile states is marked, with a particularly significant scale-up over the period 2006/07–2007/08 (£20.1–£54.9 million).

We might therefore reasonably conclude that DFID's policy commitment to scale-up programmes in fragile states was backed by resources, both in overall terms and in the education sector more specifically.

Why did DFID decide to scale-up support to education in fragile states?

I believe there are three reasons why DFID decided to scale-up support to education in fragile states: (i) to focus UK resources on where they could best accelerate progress towards the MDGs, and to get others to do likewise; (ii) to support broader processes of peace-building, state-building and poverty reduction in fragile states; and (iii) to protect UK national interests.

Focusing UK resources on where they could best accelerate progress towards the MDGs

Attention to fragile states is critical for the achievement of the MDGs. This is a fact. Not a single MDG has been achieved in any fragile state (World Bank, 2011). In 2005 – the year that DFID published its policy paper on fragile states – 14 per cent of the world's population lived in fragile states, but they represented 35 per cent of the world's poor (MDG 1), 44 per cent of maternal deaths (MDG 5) and 51 per cent of children dying before the age of five (MDG 4) (Colenso, 2005). In the latest available figures, 28 million out-of-school primary school age children – 42 per cent of the total – live in conflict-affected and fragile states (UNESCO, 2011).

The data is clear, and has been compelling in persuading DFID ministers across Labour and Coalition government administrations that if the United Kingdom is serious about making progress on MDG targets, this will require a greater focus on fragile states, including the allocation of more resources.

The 2005 DFID Fragile States policy paper included analysis that aid to fragile states had hitherto been: (i) less than half of that to better performing countries, on a per capita basis (Mackinnon, 2003); (ii) more volatile than that to better performing countries (Dollar & Levin, 2005); and (iii) in the context of post-conflict fragile states, well below absorptive capacity (Collier & Hoeffler, 2002). Significantly, the policy paper also noted that fragile states have appeared to be 'under-aided', even against a performance-based aid allocation model (Dollar & Levin, 2005).

Based on a literature review and statistical modelling, Jones and Kotoglo (2005) compared actual aid allocations (1998–2003) with optimal approaches implied by the literature. The authors used two bases for estimating optimal allocations: a need element, based on poverty and population measures, and empirical analysis of a country's capacity and effective use of aid (using CPIA scores). They found that there is a general bias against large countries, but that the influence of the policy and institutions variable is dwarfed by population and poverty/income measures. For fragile states, 'donor orphans' include a belt of countries in west and central Africa, plus Uzbekistan, and 'donor darlings' include Guinea, Papua New Guinea and Sierra Leone.

For Africa, Nigeria was by a large margin the most under-aided country. The authors concluded that the core problem for fragile states was not inappropriate models but the lack of a coordinated framework for cross-country allocations, particularly for bilateral donors (Jones & Kotoglo, 2005).

It seems therefore that there has been a strong case for allocating more aid to fragile states, on both a needs and performance basis. These arguments have been highly influential for DFID ministers across different administrations. Similar analysis for the education sector specifically has underpinned Save the Children's campaign to influence donors to allocate more aid to education in fragile and conflict-affected states (Save the Children, 2009). Over 2007 and 2008, DFID conducted an internal review of its education portfolio, to determine whether education resources were being allocated and delivered to achieve best results and value-for-money. We constructed a resource

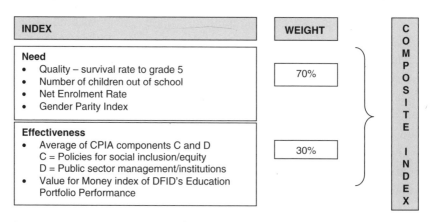

Figure 3.4 Education resource allocation model designed for DFID's Education Portfolio Review (DFID, 2009a)

allocation model to test whether DFID country programme allocations were indeed being allocated appropriately to meet the education MDGs.[8] A composite indicator (see Figure 3.4) based on indicators of need and likely effectiveness of resources for the education sector was used to identify an 'ideal' expenditure pattern – both across all countries where DFID has a bilateral programme, and across DFID priority countries listed in DFID's then Public Service Agreement with Her Majesty's Treasury.

Comparing DFID's plans at that stage for 2010/11 with these two alternative expenditure patterns showed that DFID's planned spending across countries was indeed well aligned to need, including to fragile states, principally because of planned large increases in high-population fragile countries such as Nigeria, Democratic Republic of Congo and Pakistan (and existing high levels of spending in India and Ethiopia). In its March 2010 Education Strategy – launched under the then-Labour government – DFID committed to spending around half of its bilateral education aid in fragile states (DFID, 2010a).

The new Conservative/Liberal Democrat UK Coalition Government elected in mid-2011 has not – as of this writing – published overall expenditure plans for education nor for other sectors for the current five-year expenditure period to 2015, but cursory analysis of country Operational Plans published in May 2011 show major expenditure on education in fragile states, including: Pakistan (£645m), Ethiopia (£343m), Bangladesh (£172m) and Nigeria (£143m).[9] For aid agencies advocating for increased resources to education in fragile states, this is encouraging news.

There are also signs that other donors may be putting more resources into fragile states. The Global Partnership for Education (GPE – formerly the Education Fast Track Initiative) has identified fragile states as one of three policy priorities going forward.[10] DFID has aimed to 'crowd in' financing into the GPE – in part to focus more aid on low-income countries and fragile states – making a 2010/11 commitment of £100m to the GPE conditional on matching funds from others to a ratio of £5m from other donors for every £1m from the United Kingdom.[11]

Supporting broader processes of peace-building, state-building and poverty reduction in fragile states

This argument has been influential in DFID on three levels. First, that broad investments (not just education) in fragile and conflict-affected states can support processes of peace-building, state-building and poverty reduction. Second, that this will in turn have beneficial effects on neighbouring states. Third, that investments in education specifically have the potential to improve social cohesion and support processes of peace-building and state-building.

That broad investments (not just education) in fragile and conflict-affected states will support processes of peace-building, state-building and poverty reduction has been a central tenet of the 2005 DFID policy paper on fragile states and the recent refresh of DFID's approach to fragile and conflict-affected states.

Perhaps the clearest endorsement of the collective donor understanding of the focus on state-building was Principle 3 of the OECD DAC's (2005). *Principles of Good International Engagement in Fragile States*, which maintains that development assistance should '. . . focus on state-building as the central objective'. However, many commentators – not least of all those adopting a critical theory perspective – question both the limits and motives of donor agencies in 'state-building', and the evidence underpinning the assumption that aid can support state-building. Scott (2007), for example, claims that there is little empirical evidence underpinning this assumption: 'Very little research has been done that attempts to identify successful state-building and then analyse factors that facilitated transitions from weak to effective statehood' (p. 9).

DFID's (2010b) recently published approach to *Building the State and Securing the Peace* brings together four objectives:

1. Support inclusive political settlements.
2. Address causes of conflict and build resolution mechanisms.
3. Develop state survival functions (a basic level of functionality including security, revenue, rule of law).
4. Respond to public expectations (including provisions of basic services such as education).

The interplay of these four objectives is suggested in Figure 3.5.

The second level of this argument is that supporting stability and prosperity in fragile states will in turn have beneficial effects on neighbouring states. Again, this argument has been, and continues to be, influential in DFID. Collier (2007) claims that the annual cost of one new conflict to the country and its neighbours is over $64 billion and that civil war reduces the affected country's growth by 2.3 per cent per year. Miguel et al. (2004) reinforce the cyclical nature of this problem; they claim that a negative growth shock of 5 per cent increases the likelihood of conflict

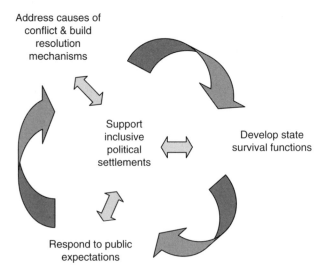

Figure 3.5 DFID's 'integrated approach' to state-building and peace-building (DFID, 2010b)

by 50 per cent the following year, with concomitant spillover effects for neighbouring countries.

The third argument that has been influential in DFID is the proposition that education specifically has the potential to improve social cohesion and support processes of peace- and state-building. There is some empirical evidence from OECD countries to support this proposition, although commentators have reached different conclusions.

Putnam (2004) cites empirical evidence from OECD countries to claim that *quantity* of education alone (i.e. aggregate years of schooling) is strongly associated with social cohesion. In contrast to Putnam, however, Green and Preston (2001)[12] claim that, while there appears to be no significant correlation at national level between aggregate levels of education and social cohesion, *inequality* of educational outcomes, however, is closely connected to income inequality, which is closely connected to many of the measures of social cohesion. In other words, it is not the total *amount* of education that is significant, as per Putnam's claim, but the *distribution* of education outcomes.

The significance of inequality is reinforced by analysis of empirical data from developing countries, with particular relevance for education. Stewart (2000) argues that civil wars occur when groups mobilize against each other, often on the basis of ethnicity or religion, and that such mobilization is effective where there are substantial horizontal inequalities (e.g. inequalities between ethnic groups) that cause resentment. 'Equality of access in education is particularly important since this contributes to equity in income earning potential, while its absence perpetuates inequality in incomes' (Stewart, 2000).

Based on cross-country regression analysis, it has been estimated that each year of education reduces the risk of conflict by 20 per cent, with secondary education found to be particularly important for promoting state 'turnaround' (Chauvet & Collier, 2005; Meagher, 2005).

The evidence supporting links between education and social stability in developing countries is by no means conclusive. It remains a contested area, where further research is needed. It is an argument, however that is continually invoked by political leaders – particularly in the United Kingdom and the United States – to justify investments in fragile and conflict-affected states, particularly those associated with the growth of radicalization and the spread of international terrorism.

Protecting UK national interests

The UK government has in recent years justified a rising aid budget on two grounds: moral duty and national interest. This twin defence of aid has been adopted both in the final years of the Labour Party administration (see, e.g., DFID, 2009b), and then more explicitly by the Conservative/Liberal Democratic Coalition government. Defending increases in the UK aid budget at the 2011 G8 Summit in Deauville, France, Prime Minister David Cameron put forward this twin argument:

> If you are not convinced that it is right to vaccinate children against diarrhoea, to try and stop preventable diseases, and to try and save mothers in childbirth, if that does not do it for you, what about this argument? That these countries that are broken, like Somalia and Afghanistan, if we don't invest in them before they get like that, we end up with the problems; we end up paying the price with the terrorism, the crime and the mass migration and the environmental devastation.[13]

This narrative has been particularly prominent in the post-9/11 era, particularly to justify engagement and increased investment in the Afghanistan/Pakistan region. This has prompted concern from others over policies combining development assistance with diplomacy and defence interests (see e.g. Beall et al., 2006; Sen, 2008; Sen & Morris, 2008).

> . . .it is easy to fall in line with a strong security oriented definition [of fragile states] because it preys on real fear and is supported by strong discourse, and policies linking defence and diplomacy interests of nations with development assistance in the war against terrorism. (Sen, 2008: 2)

Pureza (2006) argues for the need to deconstruct definitions of fragility and fragile states, and to clarify the ideological political and economic dimensions that lie behind the concept. Novelli (2010) points to an increasing militarization of aid to education, whereby aid (including for education) is increasingly bound up in military/diplomatic/development strategies and delivery mechanisms.

Focusing on the United States and the United Kingdom, Novelli critiques the notion of 'education as counterinsurgency', pointing to: USAID's June 2008 '3-D approach' of defence /diplomacy/development; Colin Powell's reference to NGO staff: '. . . a force multiplier for us, such an important part of our combat team'[14]; and former UK Prime Minister Gordon Brown's September 2009 speech on Afghanistan linking education to a 'hearts and mind' strategy. Novelli contends that the increasing militarization of aid has detrimental effects not only for long-term development progress but also for the personal security of development workers.

The defense of the aid budget on the grounds of national security has been increasingly invoked by the UK Coalition Government, as they defend to the UK taxpayer, and a hostile section of the national press, a rising aid budget in the face of cuts to domestic expenditure and services. It is not an easy task. However, it is to the credit of the three major political parties in the United Kingdom that the increase of the overseas aid budget is a task to which they are, as I write, equally committed. And that this budget is increasingly focused on where it is most needed: fragile states. This can only be good for education.

Conclusion
Zuki Karpinska

This case study concludes that an important, if not the most important, determinant of donor commitment to a country or region is protection of national interests. Suhrke and Buckmaster (2005) argue that, contrary to popular belief, the CNN effect – that is, the idea that once media attention to and coverage of crises taper, so does humanitarian aid allocation – is grossly overemphasized. Donors act according to their own interpretation of a policy discourse, appropriated and adapted to their interests.

The 'fragile states' rhetoric – outlined in this case study – is not without its limitations. 'The resilience of fragility, despite international engagement, does suggest that external actors should limit their ambitions, as new principles and policies for support to fragile situations are not magic bullets circumventing the serious obstacles that work against turnaround' (Engberg-Pedersen, 2008: 43). In a country with weak institutions and weak legitimacy, even the capacity of the fragile state government to manage donor funds hinders progress toward change. Change in these contexts will require years – if not decades – of donor commitment, and that is only if agreement on policy and institution building may be reached with the officials in power, who may themselves have short tenures in their positions.

The deadline for meeting the MDG targets will soon pass. Presumably, the Millennium Declaration will be re-packaged and re-confirmed with a further-off target date. But will the failure to meet the MDG deadline also result in a failure to renew commitment to fragile states?

Chapter 2 was a case of a global aid framework, and this chapter highlighted a donor policy. Such frameworks and policies give direction to strategists in the planning process, direction both in terms of change theory (i.e. what do aid agencies want as an end result) and budget allocation (i.e. where do aid agencies want to see this change). Although these frameworks and strategies comprise the discursive context in which humanitarian aid takes place, planners recognize that further contexts shape whether and how changes occur. The institutional culture of a given agency is one such context: the mandate, agenda and procedures peculiar to a given agency. Another such context is that of practice: the particular circumstances in which educational programming in situations of instability occurs.

Once filtered and contextualized through the different planning levels, agency decisions may sometimes appear arbitrary. However, as this case study illustrates, significant time, research and debate takes place in order to shape an agency's theory of change. When resources follow policy, there is the hope that the beneficiaries of aid will be the drivers of this change. And societal transformation without adequate investment in quality education is unthinkable.

Key questions

- To what extent has the policy discourse on fragile states translated into action for state-building and transformation?
- How can the education sector be harnessed to effect social change?
- How do donor priorities influence humanitarian action?

Notes

1 His Excellency Pierre Nkurunziza, President of Burundi, Doha, 30 November 2009, cited in Colenso, 2011.

2 In 2005, I conducted a keyword search of four academic databases, screening for articles relevant to two or more of the following categories: 'education', 'fragile states', 'aid'. It yielded no returns, although I found sixty-seven relevant records in total for 'education' and 'reconstruction'.

3 This commitment included: financial support to UNICEF; support for the Education Cluster managed by UNICEF and Save the Children; and increased resources for education in fragile states through DFID's bilateral programme.

4   Reply to Oral Question #123724 from Mr David Evennet MP (Bexleyheath & Crayford), 28 February 2007.

5   At the time of writing, DFID has not yet published expenditure data beyond the financial year 2009/10.

6   To estimate total DFID bilateral aid in fragile states, I have used DFID's database (http://www.dfid. gov.uk/About-DFID/Finance-and-performance/Aid-Statistics/), selected those countries listed as 'fragile states' in the 2005 DFID policy paper and calculated the total, and then added a share of 'regional support' (using the share of country support that can be categorised as 'fragile states' and applying that to the regional figures).

7   As a comparator, total bilateral aid to health rose from £231 million in 2001 to £708 million in 2009; over the same period, bilateral aid to health in fragile states rose from £116 million to £379 million. The share of the total bilateral health programme going to fragile states showed only a marginal increase, rising from 50 per cent of the portfolio to 53 per cent.

8   The model was constructed and the data analysed by my colleagues James Bianco and Sarah Hawkes.

9   http://www.dfid.gov.uk/Media-Room/Publications/

10 See for example, http://www.educationfasttrack.org/news/239/177/Bob-Prouty-Outlines-New-Orientations-for-the-EFA-FTI-Partnership/d,Whats%20New/

11 http://www.educationfasttrack.org/news/208/177/UK-Renews-Pledge-of-100-million-for-EFA-FTI-Challenging-other-Donors-to-Match-Funds/d,Whats%20New/

12 Green and Preston's work on social capital and social cohesion is further developed in Green et al. (2003).

13 UK Prime Minister David Cameron at the G8 Summit in Deauville, France, reported in *The Guardian*, 28 May 2011.

14 Former US Secretary of State Colin Powell, 'Remarks to the National Foreign Policy Conference for Leaders of Nongovernmental Organizations', at http://avalon.law.yale.edu/sept11/powell_brief31.asp

Further reading

Brannelly, L., Ndaruhutse, S. and Rigaud, C. (2009), *Donor's Engagement – Supporting Education in Fragile and Conflict-Affected States*. Paris: UNESCO International Institute for Educational Planning.
   A report that examines the changing nature of donors' engagement in supporting education in fragile and conflict-affected states, outlining lessons learned and emerging good practice.
Department for International Development. (2005), *Why We Need to Work More Effectively in Fragile States*. London: DFID.
   A key DFID policy paper on state fragility.
Mcloughlin, C. (2010), *Topic Guide on Fragile States*. Birmingham, UK: Governance and Social Development Resource Centre.

An annotated list of publications related to fragility. This resource guide introduces some of the most topical literature on the causes, characteristics and impact of state fragility and the challenge of aid effectiveness and lessons learned from international engagement in these contexts.

World Bank. (2011), *Conflict, Security and Development*. World Development Report 2011. Washington, DC: World Bank.

An authoritative publication addressing the devastating impacts of cyclical conflict, violence and insecurity, the central message of which is that strengthening 'legitimate institutions and governance to provide citizen security, justice and jobs' is crucial to breaking cycles of violence.

References

Andersen. L. (2008), 'Fragile states on the international agenda', In L. Engberg-Pedersen, L. Andersen, F. Stepputat and D. Jung (eds), *Fragile Situations Background Papers*. DIIS Report 2008:11. Copenhagen, Denmark: Danish Institute for International Studies.

Beall, J., Goodfellow, T. and Putzel, J. (2006), 'Introductory article: on the discourse of terrorism, security and development.' *Journal of International Development 18*(1), 51–67.

Berry, C., Forder, A., Sultan, S. and Moreno-Torres, M. (2004), *Approaches to Improving the Delivery of Social Services in Difficult Environments*. Poverty Reduction in Difficult Environments Working Paper 3. London: DFID.

Branchflower, A., Smart, M. and Hennell, S. (2004), *How Important are Difficult Environments to Achieving the MDGs?* Poverty Reduction in Difficult Environments Working Paper 2. London: DFID.

Brannelly, L., Ndaruhutse, S. and Rigaud, C. (2009), *Donor's Engagement – Supporting education in fragile and conflict-affected states*. Paris: UNESCO International Institute for Educational Planning.

Carlson, C., De Lamelle, J., Fustukian, S., Newell-Jones, K., Sibbons, M. and Sondorp, E. (2005), *Improving the Delivery of Health and Education Services in Difficult Environments: Lessons from case studies*. London: DFID Health Systems Resource Centre.

Chauvet, L. and Collier, P. (2005), *Policy Turnarounds in Failing States*. Oxford: Centre for the Study of African Economies.

Colenso, P. (2005), *Achieving the Education Millennium Development Goals in Fragile States: What is the role of aid?* Critical Analytical Study submitted for the Professional Doctorate of Education, University of Sussex.

— (2011), *Building a Theoretical Framework for Understanding the Role of Aid in Achieving the Education Millennium Development Goals in Fragile States*. Doctoral thesis submitted for the Professional Doctorate of Education, University of Sussex.

Collier, P. (2007), *The Bottom Billion: Why the Poorest countries are failing and what can be done about it*. Oxford: Oxford University Press.

Collier, P. and Hoeffler, A. (2002), *Aid, Policy and Growth in Post-Conflict Societies*. World Bank Policy Research Working Paper Series 2902. Washington, DC: World Bank.

Department for International Development. (2005), *Why We Need to Work More Effectively in Fragile States*. London: DFID.

— (2007), 'Delivering education beyond borders'. Press Release 5 April 2007. Retrieved 31 July 2011 from http://webarchive.nationalarchives.gov.uk/+/http://www.dfid.gov.uk/news/files/pressreleases/education-beyond-borders.asp.

— (2009a), *Education Portfolio Review*. Unpublished paper developed for the Investment Committee of DFID's Management Board.

— (2009b), *Eliminating World Poverty: Building our Common Future*. London: DFID.

— (2010a), *Learning for All. DFID's Education Strategy 2010–2015*. London: DFID.

— (2010b), *Building the State and Securing the Peace*. London: DFID.

Dollar, D. and Levin, V. (2005), *The Forgotten States: Aid volumes and volatility in difficult partnership countries (1992–2002)*. Summary paper prepared for the DAC Learning and Advisory Process on Difficult Partnerships.

Engberg-Pedersen, L. (2008), 'Fragile situations and international support,' In L. Engberg-Pedersen, L. Andersen, F. Stepputat and D. Jung (eds), *Fragile Situations Background Papers*. DIIS Report 2008:11. Copenhagen, Denmark: Danish Institute for International Studies.

Escobar, A. (1992), 'Planning,' In W. Sachs (ed.), *The Development Dictionary: A guide to knowledge as power*. London: Zed Press.

FTI Secretariat. (2007), *FTI Support to Education in Fragile States: A progressive framework*. Washington DC: FTI Secretariat.

Green, A. and Preston, J. (2001), *Finding the Glue that Can Fix the Cracks in our Society*. THES: 22 June 2001.

Green, A., Preston, J. and Sabates, R. (2003), *Education, Equity and Social Cohesion: A distributional model*. Wider Benefits of Learning Research Report No. 7. London: Centre for Research on the Wider Benefits of Learning.

INEE. (2004), *Minimum Standards for Education in Emergencies, Chronic Crises and Early Reconstruction*. Paris: Inter-Agency Network for Education in Emergencies.

Jones, S. and Kotoglo, K. (2005), *Aid Orphans and Darlings: Comparing actual global aid allocation to 'poverty efficient' allocation*. Oxford: Oxford Policy Management.

Laurence, C. and Poole, L. (2005), *Service Delivery in Difficult Environments: Transferable approaches from the humanitarian community*. Unpublished paper commissioned by MERLIN with funding from DFID.

Leader, N. and Colenso, P. (2005), *Aid Instruments in Fragile States*. Poverty Reduction in Difficult Environments Working Paper 5. London: DFID.

Mackinnon, J. (2003), *How Does Aid Affect the Quality of Public Expenditure? What we know and what we do not know*. Background Paper for World Bank's World Development Report 2004. Washington: World Bank.

Mcloughlin, C. (2010), *Topic Guide on Fragile States*. Birmingham, UK: Governance and Social Development Resource Centre.

Meagher, K. (2005), 'Social capital or analytical capability?: social networks and African informal economies'. *Global Networks* 5(3), 217–38.

Miguel, E., Satyanath, S. and Sergenti, E. (2004), 'Economic shocks and civil conflict: an instrumental variables approach'. *Journal of Political Economy 112*(4), 725–53.

Moreno Torres, M. and Anderson, M. (2004), *Fragile States: Defining difficult environments for poverty reduction.* Poverty Reduction in Difficult Environments Working Paper 1. London: DFID.

Novelli, M. (2010), 'The new geopolitics of educational aid: from Cold Wars to Holy Wars?' *International Journal of Educational Development 30*(5), 453–9.

ODI. (2005), *Harmonisation and Alignment in Fragile States.* London: Overseas Development Institute.

OECD DAC. (2005), *Principles for Good International Engagement in Fragile States.* Paris: OECD DAC.

Piciotto, R. (2005), *Striking a New Balance: Donor policy coherence and development cooperation in difficult environments.* Background paper for the Senior Level Forum on Development in Fragile States. London: King's College London and Global Policy Project.

Pureza, J. (2006), Peace Building and Failed States: Some theoretical notes. Unpublished.

Putnam, R. (2004), Education, Diversity, Social Cohesion and 'Social Capital'. Note for Discussion presented to Meeting of OECD Education Ministers, Dublin, March 2004.

Rose, P. and Greeley, M. (2006), *Education in Fragile States: Capturing lessons and identifying good practice.* Prepared for the DAC Fragile States Group Service Delivery Workstream – Sub-team for Education Services.

Save the Children (2006), *Rewrite the Future: Education for children in conflict-affected countries.* London: International Save the Children Alliance.

Save the Children (2009), *Last in Line, Last in School 2009: Donor trends in meeting education needs in countries affected by conflict and emergencies.* London: International Save the Children Alliance.

Scott, Z. (2007), *Literature Review on State-Building.* Birmingham, UK: University of Birmingham.

Sen, K. (2008), *Failed States or Failed Policies: Some donor-induced dilemmas.* Policy Briefing Paper 19. Oxford: INTRAC.

Sen, K. and Morris, T. (2008), *Civil Society and the War on Terror.* Oxford: INTRAC.

Slaymaker, T., Christiansen, K. and Hemming, I. (2005), *Community-Based Approaches and Service Delivery: Issues and options in difficult environments and partnerships.* London: Overseas Development Institute.

Stewart, F. (2000), *Crisis Prevention: Tackling horizontal inequalities.* Oxford: Queen Elizabeth House Working Paper Series.

Suhrke, A. and Buckmaster, J. (2005), 'Post-war aid: patterns and purposes'. *Development in Practice 15*(6), 737–46.

UNESCO. (2011), *The Hidden Crisis: Armed Conflict and Education.* Paris: UNESCO.

World Bank. (2004), *Making Services Work for Poor People.* Washington, DC: World Bank.

— (2005), *Reshaping the Future: Education and postconflict reconstruction.* Washington, DC: World Bank.

— (2011), *Conflict, Security and Development.* World Development Report 2011. Washington, DC: World Bank.

Leadership: Save the Children's Global Challenge

4

Katy Webley

Chapter Outline

Introduction   71

Case study   73

   Reflections on the *Rewrite the Future* campaign   82

   Rewrite the Future post-implementation   84

Conclusion   86

Introduction

Zuki Karpinska

The vision of Save the Children – the world's leading independent organization for children – is a world in which every child attains the right to survival, protection, development and participation. With Save the Children organizations in 29 countries, aid programmes in over 120 and income of US\$ 1.4 billion, Save the Children aims to inspire breakthroughs in the way the world treats children, and to achieve immediate and lasting change in their lives.

With the emergence of the Education Cluster, jointly led by UNICEF and Save the Children, the two aid agencies have become the EiE field's most visible leaders. Leadership may be defined as 'the processes of initiating, enabling, implementing, and sustaining change' (Mackenzie, 2006: 345). In order to frame these processes within the structures of the humanitarian aid industry, the following definition of leadership may be used, adapted from a study by the Active Learning Network for Accountability and Performance in Humanitarian Action (ALNAP): A leader is an individual or agency that provides a clear vision and objectives for crisis response focused on the affected population, and consensus among aid stakeholders to collectively realize both the vision and objectives (Buchanan-Smith, 2011). It is not enough, therefore, to develop a theory of change in terms of a vision and objectives. A leader – whether individual or institutional – must also be able to negotiate agreement between disparate institutions and their representatives, as well as to mobilize action.

It is also valuable to consider leadership in terms of accountability. Accountability refers to an actor's obligation to explain and justify institutional conduct to particular stakeholders. As discussed in Chapter 1, UNICEF and Save the Children are charged with coordinating humanitarian response for education in countries where crisis occurs. By serving as Cluster Leads, these institutions have pledged commitment to being the 'provider of last resort'. This means that if other institutions cannot meet the needs of an affected population, UNICEF and Save the Children are accountable for fulfilling those needs. However, first and foremost, any institution that operates within the realm of humanitarian aid is accountable to the populations that it seeks to assist. For the EiE community, these crisis-affected populations – and thus the stakeholders to whom an aid agency is ultimately accountable – would include learners, education personnel and their communities.

Yet, it is not just the gravitas of these institutions that determines their ability to effect change, but the leadership qualities of their representatives. The ALNAP study of humanitarian operations leadership found that 'the significance of personal authority [is] the determining factor of effective [individual] leadership, as opposed to the authority vested in position or status'. According to this argument, individual qualities resulting from experience are worth more than the weight of a staff member's rank within their employing agency.

The study categorizes these qualities into five categories (ibid.):

1. *Strategic leadership skills that relate to the bigger picture*: understanding of context; building consensus around a strategic vision and objectives, as mentioned; and a focus on the needs of affected populations.
2. *Relational and communication qualities*: such as the ability to listen, effectively present ideas and build effective relationships among others.
3. *Decision-making and risk-taking skills*: ability to make decisions quickly 'on the basis of incomplete, unreliable and sometimes contradictory information' and to take responsibility for them; flexibility; ability to learn from and correct mistakes.

4. *Management and organizational skills*: ability to compose a strong team and mentor its members; attention to detail; visionary and strategic skills.
5. *Personal qualities*: including integrity, self-awareness, self-confidence, tenacity and enthusiasm.

However, without the institutional backing of strong, recognized aid agencies – not least in financial terms – individuals are rarely given a 'seat at the table' to make policy decisions. Both UNICEF and Save the Children have the clout – through their operational presence in a substantial number of countries, their records of achievement and their financial resources – to effect change. Such legitimacy is central to obtaining funding for programming. For instance, USAID – a key branch of the largest donor government in the world – awards agency reputation and past performance as much as 35 per cent of total points in its assessment of Request for Applications/Proposals (RFA/RFP). The institutional standing of their employers provides individual leaders with a voice.

The case study presented here describes the development of a groundbreaking, multi-year strategy that solidified Save the Children's global leadership role in education in emergencies. This is a story of not only the leadership of an aid agency, but also that of the leadership of individuals who drove the strategy.

Case study
Katy Webley

There are 29 Save the Children organizations (SC Members) worldwide, all registered as charities in their own domestic headquarters. Over the last century many of them opened up offices in the same countries overseas, working in slightly different ways (with SC Members often reflecting the style, approach and priorities of their 'home countries') and sometimes in competing ways (with rivalry over geographic areas, sectoral specialisms or in-country relationships with government, UN and donor agencies). All SC Members were brought together under the 'Alliance' in 1977, but this had been a broad and somewhat loose coalition that allowed, and even enabled, SC Members to have their own character and their own strategic directions.

No wonder then that, in May 2003 at the Save the Children Members Meeting (a meeting of all CEOs), there was a common and loud request for a clearer sense of direction for the Alliance. It was time to have a process and a framework to guide our collective work. The then-Secretary General of the SC Alliance, Barry Clarke, thus requested a CEO Forum to develop a long-term Alliance strategy for the period up to 2020, which in turn would provide the framework for development of a tight 2005–09 work plan. An irreversible direction was set for Save the Children.

The year 2003 can be looked back upon as a turning point: the beginning of a change from Save the Children as multiple separate entities, through a unifying presence in many countries (albeit under one 'managing' member), up to today, where we find ourselves becoming one 'Save the Children International' (with harmonized systems, and a single line management and headquarters).

What were the drivers of that initial first shift? Initially, a sense of corporate survival was key – it was clear the world needed fewer, stronger NGOs, so Save the Children member organizations had to either combine or compete. Further, there were clear opportunities to strengthen our brand, our profile and our income. Clearly, if we chose to remain fragmented, we would miss out on the potential for our individual good to become our collective great – with greater impact for children. Much of the inspiration and persuasion at that time came from a few very focused, vocal and influential figures, scattered across the SC Members, who saw the unification as a way to make our work all the more effective for children.

From June 2003 to December 2003, there was a broad consultation process across the SC Members, and an agreed overall strategic goal for the Alliance emerged: *'By working together as a global Alliance we want to maximize our contribution for the benefit of children.'*

At the October 2003 Board Meeting in Geneva, Barry Clarke directed the CEO Forum, which was guided by four key principles:

1. Focus on priorities for the Alliance as a whole rather than the work of individual Members;
2. Develop a longer-term strategy to guide a five-year plan;
3. Deliver on Members' common desire for greater impact for children, clearer focus for our work together and better use of our human and financial resources;
4. Seek a higher level of practical cooperation among Members.

The 2020 Strategy to be developed by the CEO Forum was to contain three key elements:

1. Establishment of three to five global challenges with concrete and measurable results for a large number of children (these challenges were to last five years each, and together were to provide the ambition, direction and content for SC's programming);
2. Development of twenty-five strong members in key countries (this would enable the establishment of new national members to exist and work in their own countries, e.g. SC India, as well as increase their contribution to global work, e.g. SC Italy);
3. Achievement of unified representation at country level (to have one office and staffing structure per country).

As an example of major corporate change, the vision and direction was simple and clear.

This case study focuses on the first of these three key elements (what was, for the first year or so, known as the 'Global Challenge') and its contribution to the four stated key principles. And it is written from the perspective of SC UK – the second largest member and one that remained a central influence, contributor and implementer of the work.

The Global Challenge was to be the content pillar of the SC Alliance's new strategic direction. It was the element that would leverage our programming, and show the power of coherence, collaboration and focus. It was to demonstrate the value of working together – most importantly, through results for children.

Various themes were proposed for consideration as the Global Challenge – and two were concluded as ripe for proposals. One, on HIV/AIDS, was tasked to SC US and SC UK to develop. The other, on education, was to be developed by SC Norway and SC Sweden.

In SC UK, such were the levels of confidence that HIV/AIDS would be selected that I, as SC UK's Education Advisor, was advised to 'not bother' engaging in the education task. The reason was perhaps that SC UK and SC US (the bigger members) were confident about the weight behind their proposal or perhaps that HIV/AIDS was expected to win due to its higher external profile and income potential. Or it may just be that unfortunately education was considered a 'high value but low interest' topic (worthy but unexciting), as it has so often been.

So, meanwhile, what was the context and work of the SC education teams? Some three years previously, education advisors across the headquarters of several SC Members had been working together on emerging sub-themes. In particular, three working groups had been set up on early childhood care and development, education and macroeconomics and education in emergencies.

The work of the EiE group had made quite some headway. Of course, in 2000, INEE had been established after the Dakar Education for All Conference (Save the Children was one of the founding members of INEE). At the end of 2001, an Emergency Education Officer (Susan Nicolai) was recruited by SC UK's Education Advisor Marion Molteno, as a shared staff resource for the SC Alliance. Susan's position established one of the first few roles that would serve the broader SC membership and interests, rather than only working for one SC. In 2002, Susan led the SC Alliance through a mapping of its global work on EiE (which was later summarized within the EiE toolkit that was developed for staff; see Nicolai, 2003), agreement on a set of EiE principles and development of an EiE introductory training package. While there was increased collaboration and coherence on emergencies among education technical staff, it was at the same time, however, declining in importance for SC UK's directors.

The decline in interest was so perceptible that Susan and I drafted a position paper in December 2003 to lobby SC UK's Director of Policy and Programmes that the EiE work in headquarters and in countries (of which SC UK was a key actor) should be preserved and celebrated – rather than being seen as a good area for cost savings (which could only ever, it seemed, be justified by being a 'low priority among the emergency department'). I recall having lunch with my director, talking through the rhyme and reason for the work and it all ended in a rather noncommittal way. Thus, education in emergencies came very close to becoming a theme of work that would fall from Save the Children UK's 'core areas of work', as was the fate of so many other sub-themes and topics.

Meanwhile, SC Members were working on their proposals for the Global Challenge. I do not recall seeing much of the documentation on the US/UK submission on HIV/AIDS. I did, however, make contact with Oslo education colleagues and saw much of their drafting. SC Norway, leading on the education proposal, had chosen to focus the Global Challenge on 'Quality Education for Children in Crisis.' Under this overall challenge were two stated themes – education and conflict and education and HIV/AIDS. The initial five-year focus was proposed to be on 'Quality education for children affected by armed conflict'.

The proposal[1] outlined (against headings that were likely determined at the CEO Forum) and on which the case for education in emergencies had to be made was:

- External and internal analysis
- What we want to achieve
- The value added as an Alliance
- Visible/positive results (child focus, high number of children, measurable benefits for children, potential for quick and easy wins)
- SC Alliance capacity and competence
- Our global role
- Potential for media interest
- Opportunities for fundraising
- Opportunities to influence others
- How it would strengthen the SC Alliance
- The risks
- The cost and funding opportunities.

The CEO Forum met in January 2004 to look at progress across the three key themes of their emerging 2020 strategy (the Global Challenge, stronger members and unified representation). For the Global Challenge, the CEO Forum selected the education proposal. Senior managers in SC UK had underestimated both the potential of the topic and the ability of our Nordic neighbours to pitch it. The field of education in emergencies or, more specifically, 'education for children affected by armed conflict' would become central to our work across the world.

The CEOs would put forward this education proposal, alongside finalized proposals for stronger members and unified representation, for Board consideration at the March 2004 meeting and subsequently for presentation, discussion and approval at the May 2004 Members meeting. The CEO Forum also agreed that each of the three elements would be guided by what was termed a 'Key Challenge Team' (KCT), a team of senior leaders from across the Alliance.

The Alliance Chair Barry Clarke confirmed in his global communication on the strategy that 1 January 2005 would mark the 'implementation of the new strategy'.

The year 2004 was thus incredibly busy for SC staff working in education, and it was a time of tremendous highs. Tove Ramsaas Wang, the CEO of SC Norway, was selected as the Chair of the KCT for the Education Global Challenge. I was unaware of the competition or the politics behind this selection but no one would now doubt that the appointment of Tove was the cornerstone of much of the success that followed. As I enter my eleventh year with Save the Children, my overriding conclusion is that the success or failure of our strategic organizational processes mirrors the clarity with which the direction is set. This is not particular to NGOs, but can seem especially acute for them.

The KCT was then set up, chaired by SC Norway (Tove Wang) with a senior director from several other SC Members, namely US, UK, Sweden, Canada and Denmark. In later years, I represented SC UK on this KCT, and thus was part of the machinations at the centre. A core team was established at the SC Alliance Secretariat, consisting of a Global Challenge director (David Skinner), a project manager (John Rennie), a communications manager (Joe Hall) and a monitoring and evaluation manager (Barbara Pizzoni).

A lot of work needed to be done to get this Global Challenge 'fit for purpose', that is, in a state ready for launch and ready to achieve its aims. For a start, the proposed goals and sub-goals were still very vague. By early 2004, the KCT – with senior representatives from across the SC Members – was due to have its first face-to-face meeting. Susan Nicolai and I were asked to refine the Global Challenge's objectives for presentation to this group. My description of this coffee-fuelled process is not gratuitous: rather it has always struck me as a process that was technically right (empowering the right people to design the process) and particularly NGO-like (without any technology or fanfare, and a little bit casual). Susan and I met up at Giovanni's Italian deli on my street, in Tooting, South London, and we passed much of the morning over cappuccinos and notebooks. We concluded with four focus areas for objectives – around *access* to education, *quality* of education, the *protective* role of education and the *financing* of education. For each of these areas, we proposed a SMART[2] objective, provided a quantitative and qualitative reality check on the ambition of the objective and proposed programming options for Save the Children. We presented it to the group in the basement meeting room in our Farringdon office, and after some minor refining, these objectives were approved for the Global Challenge.

The framework, and these objectives, chartered the direction of the Global Challenge for the full five years and, when I reflect on the cappuccino process, I conclude it was symptomatic of the combination of trust, risk and pace that kept the Global Challenge moving forward and upward. This approach is not characteristic of all NGOs, nor indeed of Save the Children, rather it was a trait of this particular high-profile initiative and, more specifically, of the people involved, as well as of their leadership.

Over the years that followed, Tove chaired every bimonthly KCT meeting (the key decision-making forum) and every step along the way had her mark on it. In fact, as she stated, she 'shared' the meetings: not to be taken as a Norwegian mispronunciation, rather her term and style for ensuring all at the table participated and then took responsibility and action for decisions taken. And always with a regular and substantial supply of Norway's best chocolate, irrespective of the country in which the meeting took place.

The Global Challenge was always defined as a process designed to bring results for children – and so the bulk of effort had to be in programme (or beneficiary) countries. During 2004 and 2005, working groups were established to bring technical staff together to begin designing the detailed way forward for country programmes. The choice of countries for our programming proved messier than expected.[3] While various international definitions exist for the terms 'conflict' and 'conflict-affected', Save the Children also had to apply these to the reality in countries. Some countries were long-since post-conflict, such as South East Europe and Cambodia. Others had conflict in a small part of their territory, but not all out-of-school children were out of school due to conflict, such as in Indonesia. Other countries were undoubtedly conflict-affected, such as Somalia, with education obviously affected by this, but also torn apart by a whole range of other macro-challenges. And some did not want to define themselves by conflict, such as Ethiopia. In SC offices, some country directors pushed hard to be included (no matter how closely their country fit the definition of conflict-affected), some had to be persuaded and others chose not to join the campaign. In the end, twenty-two countries were selected, and a couple of others joined in the following years, with varying degrees of conflict and its impact on education.

A template for a Global Challenge 'country plan' was designed (based on the four objectives of access, quality, protection, financing) and a timeframe for development was agreed on. It was also agreed that each country would recruit a Global Challenge coordinator to work for and bring together SC Members in-country and avoid the initiative being seen as a single-member responsibility. Each country would be supported primarily through one member's head office, which would be the conduit for engagement with all members (e.g. Nepal was supported by SC Norway, South Sudan by SC UK, etc.) During 2004, groups of staff visited country programmes, explained the initiative and facilitated the development of their country plan for the five years. Regional consultations also took place in each region, to build energy and commitment across regions and senior management staff. Substantial amounts of time, and some money, was invested from the very beginning, to ensure this global initiative had the groundswell it needed. When I compare this process to similar initiatives or campaigns developed subsequently by Save the Children, it is this initial global 'harambee' that has been absent, and is so sorely missing.

A fundraising group formed and got going to define a target (the ambitious US$450 million to be raised for our programme work) and to look at how and where we would leverage this money. New innovative partnerships were proposed and pitches were made to our long-standing institutional donors. Save the Children far exceeded their fundraising target as country offices and SC Members worked well together to generate funds.

The particularly energetic communications group took off, with Joe Barrell and then Joe Hall at the helm, with innovative concepts, videos, case studies and materials produced apace. While there was no expected target for popular mobilization, the expected and achieved outreach of the communications work was impressive, and very innovative for Save the Children at the time.

A smaller group started on advocacy positions and, in July 2004, Jeff Chinook in the SC advocacy office in New York developed a paper on 'Options for advocacy objectives and strategies proposed'; again, much of what was initially proposed and discussed by few became the core of the strategy for the whole. Our advocacy was intended, and turned out, to be strong in-country (working with partners and in coalitions to improve access, quality, protection and financing of education) and at a global level (to donors, in particular, but also to UN agencies and among other NGOs).

In the second half of 2004, we took all of these ideas and developed[4] a 'South Sudan worked example for the Global Challenge', looking at programme activities, advocacy and costs under each objective, as well as constraints/risks and implications – basically testing our appetite and commitment. The excitement (as well as the nerves) was increasingly tangible.

In October 2004, under David Skinner as the newly appointed director for the initiative, a 'Business Plan' for the Global Challenge was approved, and we were good to go.

But we needed a better name. In the absence of significant branding capacity of our own, Save the Children secured some pro bono support from a flashy successful canary wharf company. It was one of my few insights into the communications sector, when we spent a day in their office to brainstorm issues, audiences and messages. With all the energy, colours and technology (and a wine bar in the middle of the office), we left feeling excited about what the company would produce. Within a couple of days we had our new name – *Rewrite the Future* – and we had some very detailed communication materials on message, tone and audience that would guide the various work and products over the years, to be disseminated to SC Member Head Offices and country programme offices around the world. SC's subsequent campaign was absent of the branding piece until over a year after start up, somewhat strangely since this so clearly started *Rewrite the Future* (and the wider SC family) off on the right foot.

The Global Challenge, or rather *Rewrite the Future,* set two launch dates – one internal and a later external launch – for the programme. The internal launch served to raise awareness, ensured country plans were developed, built the engagement of SC's thousands of staff and ensured all were positioned to speak out and scale up on this issue. We had a rotating globe on the Alliance extranet where countries around the world (as they launched during the day) posted pictures and videos, and shared the ambitious goals and objectives they were setting for themselves as well as for children in their country.

For the external launch, I led the process behind the launch publication with Frances Ellery (Save the Children, 2006a), which 'set out our stall' by making the case for the issue and outlining SC's ambitious campaign.

Different SC Members and country offices held high-level conferences, issued press releases, signed up supporters, launched our first publication and held media interviews all over the world. Our collective ambition of education for children in countries affected by conflict was known. We stated that we would:

1. Increase access to education for 3 million children;
2. Improve the quality of education for 8 million children;
3. Demonstrate the protective role of education;
4. Increase the financing of education for children in countries affected by conflict.

Much of what followed has been captured on the internet and in annual reports and publications.[5]

Reflections on the *Rewrite the Future* campaign

A vast number of reflections can be made on the campaign, but particularly notable for me are the following.

Clear intent for the challenge (as a means to an end and as an end in itself)

This was one of the stated key themes for driving coherence and direction for Save the Children as a family of SC Members that, in the earlier years, had seemed to become bedraggled. It did this, resoundingly. Every year the director of *Rewrite the Future* asked SC Members if the initiative was helping them deliver on individual and collective issues – and it was. The initiative steered collaboration in country programmes at a time when unified representation was just beginning, and it is seen as the first, and perhaps the strongest, sectoral convergence of Save the Children. It was also intended to be a theme that would deliver dramatic change for a large number of children; Save the Children continued to report on this, honestly and transparently, and made public both progress and challenges.

Choice of the right issue

Of course, as an education advisor and subsequently Head of Education, I would believe it was the right issue. However, it *was* right because it was relevant for many millions of children whose right to quality education was denied because of conflict. It was the right issue because it was inclusive and not exclusive, and it enabled many SC Members to engage as most had existing education work that they funded, a strategic commitment to continue education work and it was a priority for their 'home donors' (USAID for SC US, DANIDA for SC DK, etc.). And it was the right issue in that there was a growing global momentum regarding education in emergencies, getting close to a tipping point, and Save the Children's weight was helpful and timely.

Coherence of countries and staff

Rewrite the Future spoke with one voice. Not that we did not have arguments across Members, we did – on publications, on priorities, on positioning. But there was goodwill and commitment in plenty to work through them. It had, after all, always been clear that coherence and clarity was a compulsory expectation, and the KCT was the (internal) forum where conclusions would be arrived at.

Opportunity for countries to ride a wave

I was told by the regional director of West and Central Africa, who was formerly the country director of DRC, that – for a country programme – *Rewrite the Future* was like 'riding a wave'. A country director could join up and be taken along, be given the equipment and tools to scale-up the work for children and represent it to donors. It was a big wave, with a stated vision and multiple materials outlining the direction, with policy analysis and case studies, with sharing of learning and best practice and with fundraising back-up. It was head offices providing support to countries with energy, commitment and resources, rather than being just another email with one more request.

Advocacy targeted at donors

When we turned our attention to the policy environment, donor financing was perhaps the most obvious issue for an NGO to address. However we never expected the stark results that emerged when we probed deeper. Thanks to the curiosity, intelligence and persistence of one of our education policy advisors, Janice Dolan, we produced our first flagship publication, *Last in Line* (Save the Children, 2008), on the financing of education in countries affected by conflict. After getting the methodology peer-reviewed, going over data a million times and checking every word about each donor with each SC member – our publication was the first to lay out donor priorities and funding, and the massive disconnect with out-of-school children. In short, education systems in countries affected by conflict were the furthest from providing access to all, yet were the least likely to receive the funds. We updated and improved *Last in Line* each year, and it became a publication that the global education community used and trusted and had a significant influence. In SC UK we directed our energies particularly at the UK's DFID, launched a policy brief in late 2006 (Save the Children, 2006b) and, in the years and follow-up studies that followed, would like to claim some influence on the UK Government's strategy (Save the Children, 2010).

Leadership from the bottom and the top

The right people were given the right space to input, design and lead. It was not completely 'bottom–up', an overused and somewhat empty term thrown around – but rather it was based on sound inputs from technical staff. There was clear leadership from the top with Tove at the helm and David Skinner at the centre. Their leadership was not aligned with one SC Member over another, and their focus on results was clear. At the same time, *Rewrite the Future* was able to engage others – Jasmine Whitbread, SC UK's then-CEO (now the CEO for our new Save the Children International), regularly gave her time and presence at external high-profile meetings to articulately and passionately speak out on behalf of the initiative. In subsequent years, I have not seen another initiative, from SC or other NGOs, that has had the same level of sustained investment, global presence (across head offices and programme countries), clear and supported leadership and the empowerment of lower levels of staff that was evidenced through *Rewrite the Future*.

Rewrite the Future post-implementation

Rewrite the Future kept itself alive by continuing to reflect on its delivery against stated expectations. Just a year after our external launch, Save the Children asked the Boston Consulting Group (BCG, our favoured pro bono partner) to conduct a review of *Rewrite the Future*. Between March and May 2006, BCG supported SC to determine relevant Key Performance Indicators, revise the governance structure, develop annual planning processes and project plans, identify and solve some key issues on money management, etc. In May 2006, BCG presented a 'summary of conclusions'. Similarly, in January 2007, there was a process entitled 'Looking Ahead for *Rewrite the Future*, Organization, Resources and Objectives'. This included a reflection on 2005 and 2006 and recommendations for 2007, 2008 and 2009. These were important and symbolic processes as the Global Challenge was only one of three key elements in Save the Children's 2020 strategy, and it was also intended to contribute to the other two (stronger SC Members and unified presence in countries). This level of internal transparency and accountability kept all SC Members supportive and coherent and ensured that we, as an organization, remained focused on our commitment to children.

In 2009 *Rewrite the Future* was seen as nearing its conclusion. Although the initial 2020 strategy had discussed subsequent five-year education initiatives within the overall theme of *Quality Education for Children in Crisis*, there seemed to be little corporate appetite for another education focus.

There were other pressing needs, for SC as an Alliance and certainly for SC in the United Kingdom. Newborn and child survival was emerging as a priority area for SC UK (following suit to the SC US Saving Newborn Lives Initiative) and it offered a potential that another education initiative would not. In particular, as Jasmine, the SC UK CEO, often said, we needed an organization that did 'what it said on the tin' – that saved children. SC UK wanted to rebuild our health work that had been reduced some years previously, and use this work to better communicate to the UK public what we did around the world. And the SC Alliance wanted another campaign, one that would be bigger, save millions of lives of children, leverage far greater brand recognition and become a movement with mass popular mobilization.

Rewrite the Future was expected to deliver on its commitments, to wind down its internal architecture and seek to maintain the level and quality of work achieved. SC had built a stage for education in crisis, and education in conflict and emergencies in particular – and we were not expected to abandon it overnight – but, rather, it was clear that SC corporately could not maintain the energy and input from across departments as new priorities arose.

And so it was that this grand education initiative fell off the workplans of headquarter teams working in communications, campaigns and fundraising and returned to the traditional home of the education team. *Rewrite the Future* never properly ended as a campaign – rather staff in other teams shifted their focus and worked on other initiatives and new campaigns, while education staff around the world continued in their commitment to the work. Save the Children had exceeded some of the campaign's objectives (such as the number of children we would reach with an improved quality of education) and yet did not reach (and thus continue to work to achieve) other objectives (such as the number of new children who would receive an education due to the campaign).

And so in country and regional offices, *Rewrite the Future* became an activity to be sustained and embedded, and developed if at all possible – but there would no longer be a big wave to ride, that is, within Save the Children as an organization.

For children, however, the wave had turned the tide. The issue of education in conflict was without doubt one of the most prominent themes on the international agenda of donors and agencies working in education over the last few years. This is, of course, not solely due to Save the Children. Bilateral donors (such as the Dutch MoFA and the UK DFID) and multilateral donors (namely the World Bank) also pronounced their commitment to fragile states, which heavily focus on countries affected by conflict, with increased policy attention and funding. INEE went from strength to strength, as the home of all agencies working on this issue, and with the *INEE Minimum Standards* widely rolled out, understood and worked towards. Save the Children and UNICEF took up co-leadership of the global Education Cluster; I represented the former and assisted in the forming and storming of that role and relationship. The EFA-FTI – the financing mechanism (see Chapter 1) – adapted to the needs of fragile states in terms of planning and capacity building. The 2009 EFA meetings, convened by UNESCO, included conflict and emergencies on their agenda for the first time. And, of course, in 2011, the EFA *Global Monitoring Report* (UNESCO, 2011) – the undisputed bible for monitoring and debating progress on the EFA goals – focused on conflict as its theme. Financing for education in these conflict-affected countries has grown enormously, technical support has increased and investment has been made to support countries to plan, deliver and monitor the quality of education available to all children in their countries.

If the world does not achieve the MDG of all children accessing and completing primary education by 2015, it will be because of countries affected by conflict – much remains to be done. However the agenda will turn, in time. The issue of education in conflict may have had its time in the limelight – to the benefit of millions of children in countries around the world. Save the Children, no doubt, has played a significant role in achieving this.

Conclusion
Zuki Karpinska

The Rewrite the Future campaign – which came to a close in 2010 – was heralded as a success. Save the Children (2010) reports that, in the first four years of the campaign, the organization had 'succeeded in getting 1.4 million children into school', and improved the quality of education for more than ten million children through teacher training and innovative initiatives such as 'working with teachers and education ministries to introduce codes of conduct banning corporal punishment and other harmful practices' (pp. 1–2). The campaign continues to resonate through Save the Children's ongoing EiE work. *Rewrite the Future* cemented Save the Children's legitimacy as a humanitarian aid leader within the education sector.

An emerging theme throughout this case study was not only the leadership of Save the Children as an institution, but that of the dedicated individuals within it. People in Aid conducted a study of humanitarian leadership, interviewing a number of upwardly mobile middle and senior managers in three key NGOs active in education in emergencies, including Save the Children (Dickmann et al., 2010). Research participants overwhelmingly cited 'making a difference' as the main motivator in their work, while pay and benefits were seen as relatively unimportant. The results of this study would probably ring true for the leadership in other agencies concerned with EiE programming, as well. The responsibility that comes with the jobs in this field, the very notion that if one does one's job really well conflict- and disaster-affected populations may access educational opportunities, is humbling.

The importance of individual leadership and commitment within the field of education in emergencies cannot be overemphasized. Dedicated individuals were and continue to be the driving force behind the establishment and exponential growth of INEE: for instance, Susan Nicolai, who – in the past five years – succeeded in establishing and then leading the global Education Cluster Unit; Allison Anderson, who spent the better part of the last decade first as Coordinator of the Working Group on Minimum Standards then as INEE Director; Ellen van Kalmthout, a seasoned UNICEF professional and powerhouse on the INEE Steering Group, and now the global Education Cluster Coordinator; Rebecca Winthrop, former-Head of Education at the International Rescue Committee and now Fellow and Co-Director of the Center for Universal Education at the Brookings Institution; not to mention Katy Webley herself, a long-time Save the Children UK staff member who has held posts such as global Head of Education . . . These and other individuals have lent their skills and leadership to putting education in emergencies on the map. An influential *Rewrite the Future* publication, *The Future Is Now: Education for Children in Countries Affected by Conflict*, states: 'Prior to the launch of the campaign, many key [institutional] actors believed it was too complicated for education to be delivered in countries affected by conflict. This is no longer the case' (Save the Children, 2010: 2). The responsibility for advocacy for education as a humanitarian response is shared among institutions; however, it is easy to point a finger at the individuals *within* those institutions who have tirelessly lobbied for educational provision in the harshest of contexts.

Key questions

- Is agency leadership always based on individual leadership?
- Can leadership be institutionalized? Or is it better left to inspirational individuals?
- How should aid agencies, with their high turnover rates for staff, cope with the centrality of individual leadership in affecting change?

Notes

1 Internal Save the Children document: Global Challenge on 'Quality Education for Children in Crisis'.

2 Specific, Measurable, Achievable, Realistic and Timebound (SMART).

3 Note, this is quite separate to grouping of countries for our policy work. The latter was defined by a peer-reviewed methodology and was framed around 'conflict-affected fragile states'.

4 By Jane Barry, consultant.

5 See http://www.savethechildren.org.uk/en/rewrite-the-future.htm.

Further reading

Buchanan-Smith, M. (2011), *Leadership in Action: Leading effectively in humanitarian operations.* Active Learning Network for Accountability and Performance in Humanitarian Action (ALNAP) Study. London: Overseas Development Institute. Retrieved 31 July 2011 from http://www.alnap.org/initiatives/current/leadership.aspx.

A study of leadership, specifically within the humanitarian sector, carried out in order to develop a better understanding of what effective leadership looks like, to identify the determinants of good leadership and recommend ways in which it can be fostered.

Save the Children. (2006a), *Rewrite the Future: Education for children in conflict-affected countries.* London: International Save the Children Alliance. Retrieved 31 July 2011 from http://www.savethechildren.org.uk/en/docs/rtf_full_launch_report.pdf.

The launch report for the *Rewrite the Future* campaign, outlining the ambitious programme.

Save the Children. (2010), *The Future is Now: Education for children in countries affected by conflict.* London: Save the Children.

An influential report outlining the progress of the *Rewrite the Future* campaign and other developments in the arena of education-in-emergencies, as well as highlighting the many remaining challenges.

References

Buchanan-Smith, M. (2011), *Leadership in Action: Leading effectively in humanitarian operations.* Active Learning Network for Accountability and Performance in Humanitarian Action (ALNAP) Study. London: Overseas Development Institute. Retrieved 31 July 2011 from http://www.alnap.org/initiatives/current/leadership.aspx.

Dickmann, M., Emmens, B., Parry, E. and Williamson, C. (2010), Engaging Tomorrow's Global Humanitarian Leaders Today. People In Aid and Cranfield University, School of Management. Retrieved 15 July 2011 from http://www.elrha.org/uploads/PIA%20Final%20Report.pdf.

Mackenzie, K. D. (2006), 'The LAMPE theory of organizational leadership', in F. Yammarino and F. Dansereau (eds), Research in Multi-Level Issues, Vol. 5: *Multi-Level Issues in Social Systems.* Oxford, UK: Elsevier Science, pp. 345–428.

Nicolai, S. (2003), *Education in Emergencies: A tool kit for starting and managing education in emergencies*. London: Save the Children. Retrieved 30 July 2011 from: http://resourcecentre. savethechildren.se/content/library/documents/education-emergencies-tool-kit-starting-and-managing-education-emergencies.

Save the Children. (2010), Save the Children's Education Work and Influence on the UK's Department for International Development (DFID). (Unpublished Save the Children document, March 2010).

— (2006a), *Rewrite the Future: Education for children in conflict-affected countries*. London: International Save the Children Alliance. Retrieved 31 July 2011 from http://www.savethechildren. org.uk/en/docs/rtf_full_launch_report.pdf.

— (2006b), *DFID: Aid, Education and Conflict-Affected Countries. Rewrite the Future Briefing*. London: Save the Children.

— (2008), *Last in Line, Last in School 2008: How donors can support education for children affected by conflict and emergencies*. London: International Save the Children Alliance.

— (2010), *The Future is Now: Education for children in countries affected by conflict*. London: Save the Children.

UNESCO. (2011), *Education for All Global Monitoring Report. The Hidden Crisis: Armed conflict and education*. Paris: UNESCO.

Coordination: Education and the IASC Cluster Approach in the Ivory Coast

Pilar Aguilar

Chapter Outline

Introduction	90
Case study	92
Foreword	92
Political context	93
Education context	94
UNICEF strategy	96
Coordination mechanisms	98
Funding, capacity development and advocacy for EiE	102
Education Cluster and information management	104
Intersection of the work of the GSE/Cluster and UNICEF	105
Analysis	107
Conclusions	108

Introduction
Zuki Karpinska

The Inter-Agency Steering Committee (IASC) cluster approach assigns a UN agency the responsibility of humanitarian response coordination in a given aid sector should a natural or man-made disaster occur anywhere in the world. The sole exception to UN agency cluster leadership is the Education Cluster, which is co-led by UNICEF and the NGO Save the Children (see Chapters 1 and 4).

The IASC distinguishes between the tasks and accountabilities of global clusters – coordination bodies comprising institutional representatives concerned with a given humanitarian sector, with secretariat headquarters in

Geneva or Rome – and those of country-level clusters in crisis-affected contexts. According to the IASC *Guidance Note on Using the Cluster Approach to Strengthen Humanitarian Response* (IASC, 2006), some responsibilities of the global- and country-level clusters overlap, while others differ.

In simplest terms, the global-level cluster functions as a strategic planning, technical support and information-sharing body; while the country-level clusters are accountable for ensuring an effective, well-coordinated, humanitarian operation. The global level develops standards, sets policies, identifies 'best practices' and provides guidance on activities such as needs assessments; the country level applies the standards, uses global-level policies as a basis for strategic planning, adapts 'best practices' when possible and conducts needs assessments, in addition to implementing the humanitarian response plans developed. Both global- and country-level clusters are responsible for advocacy and resource mobilization (i.e. fundraising), training and capacity building of humanitarian personnel and emergency preparedness planning. Importantly, the country-level clusters do not report to the global level: rather, country clusters report to the most senior in-country UN representative, that is, the Resident Coordinator or the Humanitarian Coordinator.

The establishment of country-level clusters may be triggered by acute emergencies, or – since the cluster approach has only been in effect for a few years – clusters may be set up in a country of on-going or chronic crisis. The country-level clusters are usually based in national capitals, and their meetings – daily, weekly or monthly, depending on the complexity and intensity of the emergency – are attended by relatively senior aid agency representatives holding positions at a sector programme manager level or above. Sub-country-level clusters are common in order to coordinate agency responses in the heart of the most affected areas.

Emergencies may be divided into phases: these may include the acute emergency phase (though there may be several instances of acute crisis in a complex emergency such as armed conflict), to post-crisis, early recovery, rehabilitation and reconstruction. Clusters may also de-operationalize, or become dormant, once the 'emergency phase' of a crisis is declared over and the relief-related activities of aid agencies are replaced with longer-term development programming.

It is important to note that the 2005 UN Humanitarian Reform process is not the first attempt at country-level coordination. 'At the country level, sectors and sectoral groups have always existed and they will continue to exist . . . The cluster approach is intended, therefore, to strengthen rather than to replace sectoral coordination' (IASC, 2006: 4).

> Within the education sector, a government-led education sector working group may choose to include in its work plan, priorities and objectives a focus on education in emergencies that is similar to work done by the cluster. Nevertheless, there is no requirement for it to do so and no formal accountability within the global humanitarian system regarding its activities. In one sense, the Education Cluster is an education sector working group, focused exclusively on responding to education in emergencies. (Global Education Cluster, 2010: 9)

The following case study describes a context, the Ivory Coast, in which a country-wide education sector working group is in place, and the space that the Education Cluster membership body creates for itself within this context. The case study also discusses the challenges and opportunities of working with governments, and the advocacy and capacity building efforts of international aid agencies on behalf of education as an emergency preparedness and response sector.

Case study
Pilar Aguilar

Foreword

Pivotal to any scheme of coordination at field level is a child rights-based approach to education (see Chapter 1). Policy-wise, what is at the foundation of coordination is a child-centred and inter-sectoral effort in education. As suggested by Santos Pais (1999):

> The holistic approach of the Convention [of the Rights of the Child (CRC, 1989)] emphasizes the importance of promoting a multi-disciplinary and cross-sectoral perspective when consideration is given to policies, programmes or actions in favour of children. The aim is to focus on the whole child and to promote the effective realization of all his or her rights. It is essential, therefore, to foster an increasing synergy amongst the various sectors which are relevant to the child's life, and prevent fragmented interventions. With a cross-sectoral and inclusive perspective the value of each specialized sectoral component will be taken into consideration, but a common context will be further promoted where complementarity and interrelationship will prevail. (p. 9)

The preceding quotation masterfully articulates the indivisibility of child rights and leaves frontline responders with a challenge: how to operationalize the CRC by adopting a child-centred approach.

Political context

According to economic surveys and dominant political opinion prior to 2000, the francophone country of Côte d'Ivoire[1] was the jewel of western Africa, a showcase of stability and development progress in a turbulent region. Nevertheless, more systematic research showed that the country's social and family structure had been shaken by the market economy and by the exclusionary conventional school system. This had, in turn, engendered a crisis of parental authority and a variety of problems connected with social instability. Thus, the social conditions for confrontation had accelerated due to the lack of political democracy and the process of marginalization of urban and rural populations (Assy, 2003).

After a period of post-election violence and a failed coup attempt, the country plunged into the Ivoirian Civil War of 2002–07, with Côte d'Ivoire effectively split into two. The North was controlled by the 'rebel' New Forces, and the South by the standing government. Côte d'Ivoire became a 'fragile state' (see Chapter 3) with an estimated population of 21 million.[2]

The country was again thrust into a political crisis as a result of violence occurring around a long-delayed presidential election, which finally occurred in late 2010. Sitting President Laurent Gbagbo and his supporters refused to acknowledge the apparent victory of candidate Alassane Ouattara. The Second Ivoirian Civil War broke out in March 2011. Unlike during the Civil War of 2002, the six million people living in the economic capital of Abidjan also suffered the ruinous consequences of this civil war. The Ivoirians were left without the possibility of seeking sanctuary in the city as they had during previous conflict situations. Thus, displaced people either looked for refuge in neighbouring countries or sought shelter inland with extended family or friends.

During this period it was difficult to tell which were the 'rebel' forces in the country as both sides of the conflict were installed in positions of political authority. Prior to the 11 April 2011 arrest of Gbagbo, two governments were de facto in place. The political environment for humanitarian aid agencies operating in Côte d'Ivoire continues to be extremely delicate. As Ouattara has enjoyed the recognition of the international community, many Ivoirian people perceive all international aid workers to be pro-Ouattara, and this perception of aid workers as biased – rather than neutral – might continue to hinder service delivery.

Education context

Côte d'Ivoire follows the French education system. Six years of primary education sanctioned by the Certificat d'Etude Primaires Elementaires (CEPE) are followed by seven years of secondary school, which culminates with the baccalaureate in the student's final year. Higher education comprises universities and technical and vocational schools (grandes écoles). The system is centralized, with the government playing a key role in curriculum planning, coordination and allocation of resources and organization of national exams through three ministries: Ministry of Education (Ministère de l'Education Nationale: MEN), Ministry of Technical Education and Professional Training (Ministère de l'Enseignement Technique et de la Formation Professionnelle: METFP) and Ministry of Higher Education and Research (Ministère de l'Enseignement Supérieur et de la Recherche Scientifique : MESRS). There are also private and religious schools and universities, which previously received some subsidies from the government. Parallel to the formal education system are the informal pre-school system and the Koranic schools dominant in the northern and south-western regions, poor neighbourhoods of big cities and areas near the border with Liberia.

As the 2011 *Education for All Global Monitoring Report* details, grievances over education inequalities in the North were at the root of the civil strife in Côte d'Ivoire over the past decade (UNESCO, 2011). The political upheaval has taken a heavy toll on education, illustrating the devastating impact conflict can have on learning opportunities as well as the vicious circle in which conflict and education can become trapped. The years of conflict have had a pervasive effect on the education system as a whole, reflected most starkly in primary education enrolment rates, which fell from 79.5 per cent in 2001–02 to 54.4 per cent in 2004–05, a drop of 25 percentage points (AfDB/OECD, 2008). As a result, the enrolment rate for this age group is now lower than it was 15 years ago.

The North in particular has suffered from on-and-off insecurity for almost an entire decade. Thus, the psychosocial support element of EiE work is essential to the recovery of the conflict-affected population: evidence shows that traumatized children have limited capacity to go through the teaching and learning process (Retamal & Low, 2010).

Schools throughout the country closed during the election period at the end of 2010, due to school buildings being used as voting sites, teachers being absent while carrying out political campaigns or parental fears of letting their children out of the house given the volatile security context. Human rights violations increased during this time, adding to the insecurity caused by population movements both inside and outside the country. While schools were supposed to officially reopen in early 2011, a call for civil disobedience launched by the pro-Ouattara coalition caused schools in the Centre, North and Western region bordering Liberia (CNO) to remain closed. As a result, it is estimated that 877,177 children missed out on 4–6 months of education (Côte d'Ivoire Education Cluster, 2011). In addition, the fear of revenge continues to plague the most affected regions, creating a need for ensuring the safety of children who attend school.

Initial survey and field observation shows that, given the impact of violence and civil confrontation, it will take some time for the standard school curriculum to be provided to the affected children, especially in the North of the country. This process may take a few months and in some cases even years.

As part of the role of aid agency coordination is harnessing information and knowledge for action, a deeper analysis is required of the evolution of the education process and its inequalities in Côte d'Ivoire. Coordination of aid interventions in Côte d'Ivoire must acknowledge the integration of partner mobilization and organization at the local and community levels, especially in the areas that were 'delinked' from the centralized educational structure of the country (MEN et al., 2007). This was the role of local NGOs such as Education pour Tous (EPT), which continued to function throughout the period of insecurity on local resources and through the mobilization of teachers, parents and communities in some of the regional education directorates (Directions Regionaux d'Education National: DREN) in the North of the country. The teachers who remained in place during the lingering crisis were complemented by a large number of volunteers, ranging from private school instructors to retired teachers, religious groups, local NGOs and former students. As the split of the country became even more protracted, these ad hoc small-scale initiatives evolved into something more structured. Eventually, a group of teachers and educational officials started channelling existing initiatives into a system and assumed coordination of this emerging arrangement of alternative service provision.

As pointed out by Chelpi-den Hamer (2007):

> The main goal [of educating children in war-affected areas] was to validate the learning which was taking place in the rebel-controlled areas and to avoid the prospect of a year with no academic progress and no formal certification of learning, the so-called année blanche. Even though the MEN announced an année blanche for the north in June 2003, there was a strong willingness to keep a certain unity in the national education system in the rebel-controlled areas and to avoid penalizing northern students more than necessary. The new objective was to go beyond the

Table 5.1 Change in Primary School enrolments per school year in the North for the DREN of Bouaké, Korhogo, Man and Odienné (Ecole pour Tous, 2006)

Year	2001–02	2002–03	2003–04	2004–05	2005–06
Number of students	588,936	186,356	359,894	318,655	329,479

Source: Chelpi-den Hamer, M. (2007), 'How to certify learning in a country split into two by a civil war? Governmental and non governmental initiatives in Côte d'Ivoire, 2002–06'. *Research in Comparative and International Education* 2(3), 195.

> provision of recreational activities and informal courses (which were aimed to keep children off the streets while maintaining a certain academic level) to favour the provision of a formal type of learning (which aimed to get credentials to keep the door open to a certain form of social promotion). (pp. 193–4)

This was a local and community-based course of action, which kept the educational process alive and was even able to rebound enrolments in a period of war, as illustrated in Table 5.1.

This experience should serve as a model and lesson learned for coordination: rather than jumpstart new forms of management, partners can revert to 'business as usual' in order to underscore and reinforce the control of educational assistance under a centralized MEN. After the split, the North practically created a parallel education system due to its 'delinking' from the MEN in Abidjan, resulting in the absence of a central educational authority and the lack of central resources. The effort displayed in the North to provide education after the split with the South, shows a remarkable local effort of maintenance and value given to education at grassroots and community levels during the years of conflict (Chelpi-den Hamer, 2007). This is a positive point of departure for continuous mobilization of a rights- and community-based approach.

UNICEF strategy

It was along these lines that UNICEF proposed a strategy where by the MEN could be involved from the initial stage in the process of rehabilitation and development of child friendly spaces (CFS) (UNICEF & University of Pittsburgh, 2004). At the operational level, CFS is the provision of primary and fundamental services in health, primary education, child care and psychosocial services, integrated into a single protective environment that is both family-focused and community-based. Centres set up as part of the CFS approach provide a safe, caring space for children where they can engage in structured recreational and educational activities, as well as have access to basic primary health and nutrition services. The centres have targeted programmes for pre-school children, primary school-aged children, youth and parents. The CFS package is meant to be mutually reinforcing: ideally, but not necessarily, every service – education, recreation, preventive mother/child health care, psychosocial support and youth activities – can be made available and tailored to the needs of the affected population. The package also includes clearly identified, but flexible spaces, supplies and training activities. Minimum standards have to be established to ensure that sufficient space and equipment is provided for each service. Non-discriminatory access for all to the 'space' and its services must be guaranteed.

UNICEF's Back to School Initiative in the country aims to provide one million students with access to quality education. Activities of the Back to School Initiative include: improvement of the learning environment, including the set-up of temporary learning spaces consistent with the CFS approach; provision of pre-packaged educational cognitive and psychosocial materials (School-in-a-Box, Recreation and Early Childhood Development Kits); psychosocial support and education for peace and tolerance support for teachers; institutional capacity development; as well as monitoring and evaluation activities.

In the conflict-affected Côte d'Ivoire context, UNICEF maintains that the psychosocial and protection activities that are required to provide effective support to child victims of violence should be integrated within the usual basic cognitive activities in the school curriculum. This strategy entailed the integration of the Social Services Directorate (Direction de la Mobilisation et des Oeuvres Sociales Scolaires: DMOSS) into this comprehensive curricular response. Contrary to what one might believe, creativity under the special conditions constructed by the unstable context becomes not only a healing mechanism, but also a learning mechanism for adaptation to the new and extreme circumstances of flight, displacement or social conflict. In addition, empowering families and communities in the healing process is essential to children's care and protection and is an important social, economic and cultural factor in child development. But, often, families are worn down by conflicts, both physically and emotionally, and face increased impoverishment.

The school in the community is the best and most visible community structure from which these child support strategies can be launched (Aguilar & Retamal, 2008). A school's great potential for sustainability should be taken into consideration in order to prevent the tendency to develop temporary structures or projects that deal with the problem of psychosocial support as a stop-gap intervention, without integrating psychosocial assistance into the more stable, long-term environment and development of school curricula.

During a recent UNICEF technical mission (Aguilar, 2011), it was agreed that – until the end of the following school year in June 2012 – the process of teacher training would integrate aspects concerning play, expression and other psychosocial and life skills into the 'usual' cognitive teacher training curriculum. To make this strategy operational, a teacher guide or instrument was developed through inter-sectorial team collaboration at the level of MEN.

Clearly, this is an opportunity to integrate scattered protection responses into a more coherent and long-term endeavour as part of the education sector and MEN action.[3]

Coordination mechanisms

The Security Council, by its resolution 1528 (2004), established the UN Operation in Côte d'Ivoire (UNOCI) as of 4 April 2004. UNOCI replaced the UN Mission in Côte d'Ivoire (MINUCI), a political mission set up by the Council in May 2003 with a mandate to facilitate the implementation of the peace agreement signed by the Ivoirian parties in January 2003. Following the 2010 presidential election and the ensuing political crisis in Côte d'Ivoire, UNOCI has remained on the ground to support the new Ivorian Government.

Evolution of the education sector working group

At first informally, the education sector working group (Groupe Sectoriale Education: GSE) was established in Côte d'Ivoire in conjunction with other sector working groups – such as the health sector working group and that for water, sanitation and hygiene – to help the MEN ensure effective coordination of aid agency interventions. The GSE also provided a platform where education aid providing institutions (i.e. 'partners') could meet, and learn which activities individual partners implemented in which locations.

In the Ivoirian context, it was difficult to raise awareness of education-related issues as well as to mobilize resources for education in an environment where donors were more willing to fund traditional, so-called life-saving interventions.

UNICEF, as lead agency of the GSE, took advantage of the gap left by the government suspension of end-of-year exams in the northern part of the country in 2004 and 2005, effectively using this crisis to catalyse the restoration of the education system in the country. UNICEF gathered all technical and financial partners to mobilize the different local actors in education (government authorities, teachers, community leaders and parents) to coordinate their respective interventions.

UNICEF organized monthly sectoral group meetings, and also more specific meetings for the practical aspects of exam organization and the return of children to school. All UN agencies were involved in the implementation of these two priority actions, even those whose mandate does not really involve education, such as the UNFPA, Food and Agriculture Organization (FAO), OCHA and WHO. Even UNOCI, the Ivorian military 'Force Licorne' and the UN Police were involved in order to address the logistics of transport and ensure security for exam copies and exam centres. This coordination allowed UNICEF to discuss policies and priorities with the government and the New Forces – not on behalf of UNICEF and its mandate – but on behalf of all partners, including the peace mission, international NGOs (e.g. Save the Children organizations and the International Rescue Committee) and even financial partners (e.g. the European Union).

The GSE's terms of reference, that is, a written statement of the purpose of the group, lists its aims as identification of needs, information sharing, training and capacity building, monitoring and evaluation, partner mapping, fund-raising and institutional support for the right to education. The GSE functions at the national level in Abidjan and in several sub-country regions.

Louise Mvono, former UNICEF chief of Education in Côte d'Ivoire, recalls[4] that, in the mid-2000s, the Government co-chaired the then-informal GSE with UNICEF. At times, UNICEF called for partners' meetings without the government representative, an education officer, because he was not comfortable speaking authoritatively on certain issues. A great challenge for aid agencies concerned with education during this time in Côte d'Ivoire was that this MEN focal person who attended the GSE meetings was not at a policy- or decision-making level within the Ministry. The government representative's role was thus mainly to facilitate communication between the partners and the government education ministries. It was Mvono's role as the representative of the GSE lead agency, that is, UNICEF, to ensure that the Government was aware of the partners' meeting agenda items and of the main outcomes of meetings. Even despite the lack of decision-making authority on the part of the GSE government representative, the simple act of information sharing helped to build trust between the Government and the education partners developing educational work beyond the 'non-governmental zone'.

Mvono writes:

> Based on my [later] experience in Zimbabwe, I would suggest, whenever possible, that Government leads the policy discussions and sets the priorities within the GSE. This group should be used by the Ministry of Education to share its vision and discuss its education priorities with all the partners at the same time. This helps to avoid a situation where the Ministry gives different priorities to different partners; it allows partners to plan and coordinate their support to the Ministry of Education in a more coherent, transparent and coordinated way; it facilitates experience-sharing among the partners; and it strengthens the Ministry of Education coordination role as they know which partner is doing what where.[5]

No regular meetings of the GSE took place in the months preceding the December 2010 elections. Those that did take place focused on Côte d'Ivoire's request to the EFA-FTI (see Chapter 1), a global partnership between developing countries and donors, to accelerate progress towards the goal of universal completion of quality primary education by 2015. Côte d'Ivoire is one of the forty-five (most recent figure at the time of this writing) countries that took part in the FTI and has a leading role.

In addition to providing humanitarian responses to the current crisis, UNICEF's Education Section has kept the FTI application process active, even during the period of acute emergency, and in spite of the movement of different donor group members (World Bank, African Development Bank and UNICEF) out of Abidjan. Distance support was provided to the national FTI Task Force in Abidjan. With the resumption of the activities of the Education Section at the World Bank recently, a World Bank high-level evaluation was conducted from 20 June 2011 to 1 July 2011 in order to accelerate the process and ensure that the Côte d'Ivoire FTI application was submitted by the deadline.

Evolution of the Education Cluster in Côte d'Ivoire

In 2008, the first Education Cluster was set up in the Zanzan region (Boundoukou) by UNICEF, DREN and Save the Children representatives with the participation of forty national educational experts.

According to Bakary Diawara, UNICEF National Education Officer in Côte d'Ivoire at that time, the sub-national Education Cluster had two main objectives. First, to identify the gaps caused by the crisis and second, to efficiently coordinate the humanitarian actions in the field. 'By establishing a sub-national education cluster we will not only reinforce and increase the regional educational interventions, but also will ensure strategic prioritization of resources.'[6]

The Education Cluster was activated once again in January 2011 following the post-electoral crisis in Côte d'Ivoire, in order to ensure an effective joint strategy and collaborative response to the crisis from international, national and governmental agencies as well as to prepare for continued and future emergencies. The Education Cluster constitutes a national Education Cluster in Abidjan, co-led by UNICEF and Save the Children, and several education sub-clusters at the sub-country regional level.

At national level, this entails coordinating preparedness, response, rapid assessment and information management activities on behalf of cluster members to avoid duplication of activities and to maximize synergies and partnerships. UNICEF and Save the Children are also coordinating the regional education sub-clusters in the West, East and South. UNICEF is responding to the needs of the immediately affected population as required by its *Core Commitments for Children in Humanitarian Action,* UNICEF's blueprint for providing a consistent response in emergencies that is predictable to governments and other stakeholders.

The purpose of establishing an Education Cluster in a country with a functioning education sector working group was that the cluster arrangement gives UNICEF a formal mandate to act as 'the provider of last resort'. As mentioned in Chapter 1, this means that the cluster lead agency is ultimately responsible for ensuring an appropriate response in a crisis, when governments and other aid agencies cannot fulfil the needs of the crisis-affected population. Prior to the establishment of the Education Cluster in Côte d'Ivoire, UNICEF played the 'provider of last resort' role within the country in an ad hoc manner, depending on the UN Humanitarian Coordinator priorities and financial capacity, as well as on the willingness of partners to accept UNICEF as the coordinating agency. The move to the cluster approach renders UNICEF accountable not only from the above programmatic perspective but also as the agency with the humanitarian mandate on child rights and education. This is important for UNICEF country offices as it makes a great difference in terms of fundraising and monitoring of rights-based approaches to education in humanitarian settings.

Since the beginning of the crisis in November 2010, the GSE only met once in June 2011, again about the FTI, on the occasion of the World Bank mission to Côte d'Ivoire. At the GSE meeting, the Education Cluster was asked to make a presentation about the state of education in the post-crisis context. However, the GSE was not fully re-activated: there is no meeting schedule or standing agenda. A current challenge is that development partners such as UNESCO take part in the Education Cluster but are not able to contribute since they are not implementing EiE activities. This is unfortunate, as UNICEF places great emphasis on primary schooling, and – as UNICEF is a major source of funding for country-level partners – partners seeking grants align their priorities accordingly. However, the Education Cluster is mandated to address early childhood development (ECD) through to higher education in crisis contexts. UNESCO could facilitate the process to expand the Ivoirian focus beyond primary education provided education funding is made available for post-primary schooling, and when the GSE is more functional than at the moment.

The MEN participates in the Education Cluster, but its representative is different than that for the GSE. Similarly, within UNICEF, two different people represent UNICEF on the GSE and the Education Cluster: one deals with the whole country; the other has a more humanitarian focus on a limited number of regions, especially the North.

Jennifer Hoffman, at the time of this writing, the Education Cluster Coordinator for Côte d'Ivoire, opines:

> The Education Cluster is currently the only functional coordination platform for the education sector. For instance, [the United States Agency for International Development] USAID's Development Advisor attended the last Cluster meeting to get information about the state of education in the post-crisis context. Should the GSE be formally re-activated, I believe there would still be a case for their co-existence as we still need to coordinate emergency interventions [the education needs of internally displaced populations and UNICEF's Back to School campaign] and the GSE does not include an emergency response focus but a policy one (FTI).[7]

Hoffman also recalls[8] that, during her previous experience in post-2010 earthquake Haiti, there were separate Education Cluster and Education Sector Group bodies, with no linkages. The Sector Group enjoyed government support and prioritization, as well as that of the development banks. Meanwhile, the government dismissed the Education Cluster as an NGO and agency endeavour.

Funding, capacity development and advocacy for EiE

The Consolidated Appeals Process (CAP) – a funding mechanism designed to attract contributions from multiple donors in protracted crises – has become the humanitarian sector's main tool for coordination, strategic planning and programming. As a planning mechanism – and not only an appeal for fundraising, as it is commonly perceived – the CAP has contributed significantly to developing a more strategic approach to the provision of humanitarian aid. As a coordination mechanism, the CAP has fostered closer cooperation between governments, donors and aid agencies, in particular UN agencies, NGOs and components of the International Red Cross and Red Crescent Movement (see also Chapter 1).

The Education Cluster in Côte d'Ivoire has been instrumental in facilitating coordination of humanitarian agencies in the education sector. Côte d'Ivoire's initial Humanitarian Appeal for education represented US$1,288,324, a figure that was reviewed and increased to US$15,581,500 as the result of an Education Cluster needs assessment and its advocacy for the importance of education.

In the Ivoirian context, the development of a new layer of coordination that is the cluster approach has reinforced the global pledging capacity and management of the CAP.

The sum total of advocacy measures of EiE partners vis-à-vis those of the Ivoirian Ministry of Education officials has resulted in great successes, of which the CAP funding allocation for education is only one of the more recent.

Working together, the partners arranged for government trainings on the fundamental *INEE Minimum Standards* guidebook (see Chapter 2) beginning in 2007. The training was expanded in 2008 for national-level representatives as well as for twenty-two regional education directors (Anderson et al., 2011).

> While initially expressing resistance to what they perceived as a 'foreign set of education rules', a number of Ministry of Education officials have a few years later become champions of education in emergencies and of the *INEE Minimum Standards*, and Côte d'Ivoire is regarded as an example in the West and Central Africa regions of the institutionalization of the right to education in emergencies. (Anderson et al., 2011)

Given her participation in the *INEE Minimum Standards* Capacity-Building Workshop in 2007, the MEN Deputy Director for Pre-school, Primary and Secondary Education was identified as the EiE focal point by her peers. This was very helpful in finding an entry point and ally within the ministry regarding all EiE issues. 'However, [EiE] is not formally written into the Deputy Director's job description and she faces difficulties in dedicating time and finding support [for it] within her hierarchy' (UNICEF, n.d.: 2).

Key Ministry of Education representatives also participated in a 2009 regional training for EiE 'frontline responders' (see e.g. UNICEF, 2006), a programme organized by the Global Education Cluster, as well as the regional Education Cluster Coordinator training in 2010. Both of these trainings presented an opportunity to learn about the planning processes concerned with and implementation logistics of education as a humanitarian response.

Such hands-on advocacy efforts resulted in a 2010 ministerial decree establishing an EiE unit within the Ministry. Such a unit institutionalized (see Chapter 2) attention to education as a humanitarian response within government structures. EiE has also been integrated into the Ministry's three-year Mid-Term Action Plan (2011–13) and ten-year Education Sector Plan (2010–20). Moreover, the government has supported the development of a national EiE strategy and development of national and regional EiE action plans.

Education Cluster high-level advocacy endeavours between the months of January 2011 and March 2011 were also integral to the reopening of schools in the CNO areas, which had been closed due to the election crisis.

Furthermore, on 17 May 2011, the Government convened a large assembly in Abidjan with all government education actors – including local education administrators, school principals, inspectors and the like. The Government invited a UNICEF representative to attend on behalf of the GSE, and allocated the time for a speech on Education Cluster priorities.

Education Cluster and information management

According to the *IASC IM Guidance*, all clusters must have an Information Management (IM) Focal Point to oversee the collection, analysis and dissemination of data and information. In practice, however, few of the country-level Education Clusters have a dedicated person to fulfil this role. The Education Cluster in Côte d'Ivoire, however, has a full-time Information Manager who participates in the OCHA-led Assessment and Information Management Working Group.

In April 2011, the Education Cluster in Côte d'Ivoire, in coordination with regional and local education authorities, had launched a formal, school-by-school assessment in the seven sub-country regions comprising the strongly affected CNO area. With the participation of all of the education partners, data on 9,907 schools out of a total of 11,118 were collected and analysed with the assistance of the Education Cluster Information Manager.

The purpose of the assessment (Côte d'Ivoire Education Cluster, 2011) was to identify the most urgent needs facing education. The timely availability of the assessment results proved instrumental in the planning, programming and implementation of the Back to School Initiative, notably to better achieve the challenging goal of bringing back to school one million children to fulfil their right to education.

The key findings (ibid.) of the assessment can be outlined as follows:

- Ninety per cent of schools have reopened throughout the CNO area.
- Most schools are not only open but also seem to be functioning. Overall, over 80 per cent of classes are being held.
- Approximately a third of teachers have not returned to their teaching positions.
- Overall, the teacher–student ratio has increased from 1:37 to 1:47.

Information from the assessment has been fed back to the Government through several channels: participation of the MEN in the Education Cluster; a formal presentation made to the Government and the World Bank delegation in the framework of the FTI request; presentation and dissemination of assessment results to regional directors and school inspectors; as well as a presentation at a national Back to School workshop. In addition, the assessment information is being shared outside of the education sector: the Education Cluster is producing a CD-ROM with all assessment data and findings; assessment information has already been shared with the Ministry of Planning in the framework of the revision of the Poverty Reduction Strategy Paper (PRSP), as well as with the Ministry of Social Affairs and Solidarity, which is the focal point for humanitarian assistance and liaising with humanitarian actors.

Based on this evidence, the Government must find an efficient and durable solution that will facilitate the access to school for all children, especially for girls.

Intersection of the work of the GSE/ Cluster and UNICEF

During the World Bank assessment of the FTI process, the national Education Cluster provided a presentation based on the main results of the assessment regarding the opening of schools following the post-electoral crisis. The national Education Cluster also shared its report on the effect of the conflict on education facilities, which highlighted 224 reported attacks since the beginning of the crisis, with the global Education Cluster and the Global Coalition to Protect Education from Attack (GCPEA). As a result, information on education in Côte d'Ivoire was integrated into the UNICEF Deputy Executive Director's presentation at an advocacy event in New York on the drafting of a new Security Council resolution establishing attacks on schools and hospitals as a trigger for the UN Monitoring and Reporting Mechanism on the six grave violations of children's rights in armed conflict (see Chapter 1).

It is possible to observe both the positive and helpful complementarity of the sector working group and/or cluster mechanisms. The FTI benefits from the Education Cluster main findings and incorporates them in its own assessment. In addition, the different UNICEF concerns have been taken into consideration and in-depth work has been done especially with regard to the boosting of equal access to education (both from a gender and regional point of view) and retention in schools: girls' education, alternative education, that is, *classes passerelles* (accelerated learning or catch-up classes), community schools and the process of integrating Islamic schools in the formal system, community-based rehabilitation and construction, etc.

The problem of sustainability of the achievements of UNICEF's and partners' Back to School Initiative is a difficult equation to resolve. We have to tackle this problem without delay so as to obtain – in a rather short period of years – a performing and autonomous educational system. In fact, the most important question is the following: In the absence of external assistance at the sub-country level of a DREN or IEP (Inspection de l'Education Primaire), how can those responsible for the education process develop into local awareness agents for schooling for all children? By means of what resources and sponsorship at the local level? The answers will constitute the foundation of activities that will rebuild and improve school education for children in Côte d'Ivoire (MEN et al., 2007: 28).

Recently, the Minister of Education herself was very clear that teachers should become 'missionaires de l'humanitaire' (humanitarian missionaries) and help to calm the social climate, support the national reconciliation process and teach children to live together peacefully. A teacher training programme being developed as part of the Back to School campaign attempts to follow and implement these policy guidelines in practice (Aguilar, 2011).

Analysis

'Business as usual' responses in humanitarian education, especially during the 'post-conflict' phase, need to be revised in order to ensure quality and to avoid reproducing the same flaws within the education system that had existed before the crisis. These flaws could very well be partly responsible in the pre-conflict situation for accelerating contradictions in society. The Rwanda experience suggests that:

> The role of well-educated persons in the conception, planning and execution of the genocide requires explanation; any attempt at explanation must consider how it was possible that their education did not render genocide unthinkable. The active involvement of children and young people in carrying out acts of violence, sometimes against their teachers and fellow pupils, raises further questions about the kind of education they had received. For those preparing educational responses appropriate to the post-genocide situation, it was clear that Rwanda's education could never be the same again; it was evident that such themes as peace, reconciliation, human rights and tolerance would have to figure in the 'values of education' of all Rwanda's children and young people in the future. (Aguilar & Richmond, 1998: 122–3)

'Business as usual' is no longer a viable option. A curriculum that does not take into account the psychosocial needs of the generation of child victims of armed conflict and natural disasters is a recipe for exclusion and future social conflict. The humanitarian dimension and content of education does not end with the formal end of conflict and/or crisis.

As seen in different situations, the transition to 'normalcy' requires a more integrated approach, including the building of bridges between rights-based educational interventions and the priorities set hastily by development bilateral agencies or the World Bank, normally at a central level in coordination with newly established and 'post-conflict' ministries of education.

Consequently, the coordinating process in the education sector should be able to take into account the long-term and unequal set of problems left in the 'post-conflict' situation. The existence of conflict-affected, vulnerable populations – such as the internally displaced, over-aged school children, traumatized populations – necessitate that the school should be a healing vehicle, rather than one more economic factor in the process of developing the table of human resources of a country. The way into the reconstruction and development process, as well as the central aim of coordination, should be a rights-based approach to education.

The Education Cluster and the Education Sector Group can synchronize their actions by working with administrative, traditional and religious authorities at regional and local levels, the national government should harmonize planning, implementation and evaluation of education policy throughout the nation. Strengthening the coordination of education policy will require a dual strategic approach.

Within the Government, there will need to be a re-strengthening of inter-ministerial collaboration, particularly between the three main ministries in charge of the educational system in Côte d'Ivoire (Education, Vocational Education and Higher Education). Coordination efforts between the three ministries must intensify in order to jointly develop an initial set of policy options and priorities as the basis for broad consultation with other stakeholders. In addition, the Government will need to reinforce channels of communication between DRENs and the central division, thus enabling the regional directors to be fully involved in the design, implementation and monitoring of budgets and funding.

This approach needs the involvement of other stakeholders, particularly parents, teachers and the business sector. Prior to and during the conflict in the North, initiatives had been taken to better engage parents through parent–teacher associations, as well as the civil society in general. This dialogue must be restored and strengthened. This was probably the basis of a successful first attempt at developing the cluster approach in Côte d'Ivoire.

The central value of a rights-based approach to education should be present in the process of reconstruction and development. A certain division of labour between 'humanitarian' and 'development' agencies and actors should not be alienated from the main rights-based approaches that should pervade both processes.

Conclusions
Zuki Karpinska

In some countries, there is a strong rationale for having a sector group and a cluster: the existence of an emergency programme in sub-country regions and development programmes in non-crisis affected regions. In other countries, the situation is so fragile that there is need to keep the cluster activated throughout the transition or recovery period, in case of recommencement of active conflict. The possible ambiguity of responsibilities and overlap of activities between different coordination mechanisms are often a response to such sudden changes in the 'phase' of the crisis situation.

In Côte d'Ivoire, there is a case for the existence of both the Education Cluster and an Education Sector Working Group, that is, the GSE, with strong cooperation between these groups and the government ministries.

However, as suggested by Mvono:

> In my personal view, based on my recent experience in Zimbabwe and the challenges that I faced, is that UNICEF, as the global cluster lead should try, as much as possible to avoid having the 2 roles (GSE/Cluster) in a country. It creates confusion among the partners and if it is not well managed, it can have an impact on UNICEF relationships with the Government or on the cluster ability to effectively play its humanitarian role. Save the Children, or another organization should play the role of cluster lead and UNICEF should continue to be a key player among the humanitarian partners but the organisation should keep a strategic position in the GSE as it is the coordination body for policy/strategy and priority discussions. Our contribution/participation in these meetings is key to influence policy orientations and really build back better.[9]

In the case of Côte d' Ivoire, the coordination processes have emerged from different phases of an extended period of conflict. The establishment of country-level clusters responds to a new UN mechanism of coordination developed at the global humanitarian level. The split between an existing mechanism like the GSE, mostly oriented to 'post-crisis development', and the Education Cluster with its distinctive 'humanitarian' role, does not have to result in weakened coordination. In fact, coordination could be strengthened through the coexistence of these two bodies, as long as the ministries of education remain meaningfully involved in – if not in charge of – both mechanisms.

> The primacy of national authorities is recognized [within the *IASC IM Guidance*] in that cluster and sector leads and OCHA are to make sure that [crisis] response information management activities support national information systems, follow standards, build local capacities, and maintain appropriate links with relevant local, regional, and national government authorities. (McDonald & Gordon, 2008: 67)

Involvement of government authorities in such coordination mechanisms would be enhanced through demonstrating the benefits of such coordination, especially in terms of information sharing. When governments see the advantages of the cluster approach for their own work, the approach has a greater chance of success at building ministry capacities to assume the coordination role once the emergency phase of a crisis has ended.

Key questions

- In what way does the IASC cluster approach add value to existing in-country sector coordination mechanisms?
- In what way can a rights-based approach inform programme strategy?
- What is the relationship between information sharing and coordination?

Notes

1 The name 'Ivory Coast' was changed to Côte d'Ivoire in 1985.
2 World Bank, Côte d'Ivoire Data, 2009.
3 See http://www.unicef.org/infobycountry/cotedivoire_58569.html.
4 Personal exchange with Louise Mvono, Chief Education Programme, Khartoum, July 2011.
5 Ibid.
6 Personal exchange with Bakary Diawara, UNICEF Education Specialist, Congo Brazzaville, July 2011. Also, see http://www.rezoivoire.net/news/region/1154/l-unicef-installe-le-groupe-sectoriel-education-du-zanzan.html.
7 Personal exchange with Jennifer Hoffman, Education Cluster Coordinator, Côte d'Ivoire, July 2011.
8 Ibid.
9 Personal exchange with Louise Mvono, op. cit.

Further reading

Aguilar, P. and Retamal, G. (2008), 'Protective environments and quality education in humanitarian contexts'. *International Journal of Educational Development* 29, 3–16.
    An informative article on the role of schools as protective environments for conflict-affected children and the benefits of a humanitarian curriculum that addresses psychosocial needs.
Global Education Cluster. (2010), *Education Cluster Coordinator Handbook*. Geneva: Global Education Cluster. Retrieved 31 July 2011 from http://kg.humanitarianresponse.info/LinkClick.aspx?fileticket=EKNLvcng4CI%3D&tabid=70&mid=425.
    A comprehensive handbook on Education Cluster operations at the country-level, complete with step-by-step guidance on fulfilling the many responsibilities of the Cluster Coordinator position.
IASC. (2006), *Guidance Note on Using the Cluster Approach to Strengthen Humanitarian Response*. Geneva: Inter-Agency Standing Committee.
    A short, authoritative statement of the responsibilities of Clusters, both at global and country levels.

Sany, J. (2010), *Education and Conflict in Côte d'Ivoire*. Special Report 235. Washington, DC: United States Institute of Peace. Retrieved 31 July 2011 from http://www.usip.org/files/resources/SR235Sany_final_lowres-1.pdf.

A report on the relationship between conflict and education in Côte d'Ivoire, suggesting policy and programming approaches for this context and other crisis-affected situations.

References

AfDB/OECD. (2008), Côte d'Ivoire. *African Economic Outlook*. 257–70. Retrieved 30 July 2011 from http://www.afdb.org/fileadmin/uploads/afdb/Documents/Publications/30727906-EN-COTEDIVOIRE-AEO2008.PDF.

Aguilar, P. 'Back to School Initiative in Côte d'Ivoire' (unpublished UNICEF document, Mission Report, 27 June 2011).

Aguilar, P. and Retamal, G. (2008), 'Protective environments and quality education in humanitarian contexts'. *International Journal of Educational Development 29*, 3–16.

Aguilar, P. and Richmond, M. (1998), 'Emergency educational response in the Rwandan crisis', in G. Retamal and R. Aedo-Richmond (eds), *Education as a Humanitarian Response*. London: Cassel.

Anderson, A., Hoffman, J. and Hyll-Larsen, P. (2011), 'The Right to Education for Children in Emergencies'. Unpublished draft.

Assy, E. P. (2003), 'Dynamique socio-économique et crise familiale et éducative en Côte d'Ivoire de 1960 à 1990'. *Revue Internationale de l'Education. 49*(5), 433–62.

Chelpi-den Hamer, M. (2007), 'How to certify learning in a country split into two by a civil war? Governmental and non governmental initiatives in Côte d'Ivoire, 2002–2006'. *Research in Comparative and International Education. 2*(3), 191–209.

Côte d'Ivoire Education Cluster. 'Back-to-school in Côte d'Ivoire: an assessment one month after the reopening of schools in the CNO area'. (Unpublished UNICEF document, 5 May 2011).

Global Education Cluster. (2010), *Education Cluster Coordinator Handbook*. Geneva: Global Education Cluster.

IASC. (2006), *Guidance Note on Using the Cluster Approach to Strengthen Humanitarian Response*. Geneva: Inter-Agency Standing Committee.

McDonald, B. and Gordon, P. (2008), 'United Nations' efforts to strengthen information management for disaster preparedness and response', in S. Amin and M. Goldstein (eds), *Data Against Disasters*. Washington, DC: World Bank.

MEN, UNICEF and European Commission. (2007), *Rapport final – Atelier d'évaluation à mi-parcours de la campagne nationale pour le retour et le maintien des enfants / filles à l'école 2007*. Abidjan: MEN.

Retamal, G. and Low, M. (2010), 'Humanitarian curriculum and psychosocial interventions: an annotated bibliography'. *Prospects 40*, 535–57.

Santos Pais, M. (1999), *Human Rights Conceptual Framework for UNICEF*. Innocenti Essays No. 9. Rome, Italy: UNICEF International Child Development Centre. Retrieved 31 July 2011 from http://www.gddc.pt/direitos-humanos/temas-dh/pdfs/essay-9.pdf.

Sany, J. (2010), *Education and Conflict in Côte d'Ivoire.* Special Report 235. Washington, DC: United States Institute of Peace. Retrieved 31 July 2011 from http://www.usip.org/files/resources/ SR235Sany_final_lowres-1.pdf.

UNESCO. (2011), The hidden crisis: Armed conflict and education. *Education for All Global Monitoring Report.* Paris: UNESCO.

— (n.d.), 'Côte d'Ivoire: Integrating EiE in Education Sector Planning' (unpublished UNICEF document).

— (2006), *Education in Emergencies: A Resource Tool Kit.* A Publication of the Regional Office for South Asia in conjunction with New York Headquarters. Retrieved 31 July 2011 from www.unicef.org/ rosa/Rosa-Education_in_Emergencies_ToolKit.pdf.

UNICEF and University of Pittsburgh. (2004), Child Friendly Spaces/Environments (CFS/E): An integrated services response for emergencies and their aftermath. Pittsburgh, PA: UNICEF/ University of Pittsburgh.

Relief to Development: Community-Based Education and State-Building in Afghanistan

6

Sara Bowers Posada and Rebecca Winthrop

Chapter Outline

Introduction 113

Case study 114

   Rebuilding education amid an uncertain future: insights from
the ABEC and PACE-A Consortia 116

Conclusion 126

Introduction

Zuki Karpinska

The idea that relief aid must be tied to longer-term development efforts is well-established in the humanitarian aid industry. A recent article on impediments to humanitarian aid provision divides 'emergency response' into 'two stages: the life-saving/sustaining response and the self-sufficiency response' (Thevenaz & Resodihardjo, 2010: 16). During the first, aid-affected populations have access to essential services (core humanitarian aid sectors of food and water, health and shelter) and no longer experience life-threatening conditions; during the second, conflict-affected populations 'are no longer dependent on outside help to survive' (ibid.).

The notion that relief and development follows a continuum (see, e.g., Buchanan-Smith & Maxwell, 1994) with a discrete beginning, that is, the acute emergency phase, and a discrete end, that is, the continuation of efforts to improve livelihoods, has been discredited. In complex emergency, chronic crisis and even natural disaster contexts, this progression is rarely linear; 'progress might be "backwards" (towards crisis rather than progressing away from it)' (Maxwell et al., 2008: 55–6).

The case study in this chapter presents a longer-term education programme operational within the evolving nature of the conflict in Afghanistan: 'post-conflict' to 'pre-conflict' to resurgence of conflict. Likewise, the aid agency perspectives of relief and development approaches during the implementation of the programme shifted from humanitarian relief, to post-conflict rebuilding with a state-building element, to conflict-sensitive programming with operations in full-scale war. Far from a 'relief-to-development continuum', the Afghan context is a case of a protracted and complex crisis, characterized by iterative processes of taking steps forward and back.

Case study

Sara Bowers Posada and Rebecca Winthrop

Modern education systems are the responsibility of the state, leading to standardized public education in most countries. At the same time, children's needs and community desire for education frequently leads to more localized responses – whether for reasons of quality control, religious proclivity or state failure to provide education for all children. In Afghanistan, the role and scope of community-based education has responded to state capacity, or lack thereof. In the first decade of the new millennium, NGOs designed community-based education programmes to respond to community needs, donor priorities and a rapidly changing context.

Community-based education, in which schools are supported by communities and NGOs in villages where there is no access to government-run schools, is a local solution, reliant on local people to teach, monitor schools and support teachers. It is particularly suited to conflict-affected, conservative and rugged Afghanistan. First, community-based education was developed and refined in unstable communities and in refugee camps during the country's decades-long conflict – whereby local and international NGOs took their cues from and supported resourceful and courageous community members who resisted the Taliban's ban on girls' education by offering to educate girls, and boys, secretly in their homes. Parental concerns about safety in conflict-affected communities meant that smaller, nearby schools held in mosques and in the homes of trusted neighbouring families presented an attractive option. Children are less exposed to danger when they only have to walk short distances within their own communities. At the same time, fragile states engaged in conflict have fewer resources to build and run schools, leaving a vacuum to be filled by local responses. In the case of Afghanistan, girls were explicitly not allowed to attend school during the Taliban era.

Afghan culture values protecting girls' honour by keeping them safe at home and, in many cases, out of school. Though parents value education highly, concerns about security keep many Afghan girls confined to the home or their immediate locality. As girls age, their mobility is further restricted. Community-based schools serve as a more trusted option for families than distant schools operated by strangers where girls' security may seem to be threatened. Finally, community-based schools respond to the needs created by Afghanistan's incredibly remote and rugged terrain. It is challenging for students to travel to other villages to attend school, and it is challenging for a state with low capacity to set up a structurally sound and official 'modern' school in each remote hamlet.

Numerous international and national NGOs increased their education activities after the initial overthrow of the Taliban in 2001. International press highlighted the inability of girls to attend school under the former regime; Afghan children's, especially girls', access to education became a favoured cause in the initial post-conflict era. Addressing girls' education was a way for international actors and the public to fix some of the worst injustices perpetrated under the Taliban. Aid funding flowed to education from multilateral, bilateral and private sources. Demand for education on the part of Afghans was immense. In every village where Catholic Relief Services (CRS) worked throughout western and central Afghanistan, for example, villagers unfailingly asked for assistance to educate their children.

In this case study we examine the range of issues that confront education planning and programme design in a context that is moving from relief to development. To do this we use the prism of two consortia of NGOs focused on rejuvenating Afghanistan's education sector in the mid-2000s. We discuss these consortia as former participants. With little proven good practice on how to rebuild education systems as they transition out of war, the NGO consortia faced multiple questions, including: What is the best way to ensure that education progress and NGO work contributes to state-building and peacebuilding? Are there cases where aligning with or supporting new government education policies would not be acceptable or in the best interest of peace building efforts? How do NGO operations move from employing the strategies and tactics appropriate for an emergency and relief context to those better suited to a development context?

Rebuilding education amid an uncertain future: insights from the ABEC and PACE-A Consortia

Tracing the trajectory of two education consortia, made up of international NGOs and funded by external aid donors, highlights a range of important design issues that must be considered when developing programmes in a context of transition. The NGO teams grappled with deciding how best to coordinate with Ministry of Education (MoE) counterparts as well as which role and responsibilities each actor had to assume in order to build lasting government capacity. Within this, specific issues of whether to pay teachers' salaries and whether to follow the school construction guidelines set by the government were particularly rich for debate. Additionally, the teams debated a range of issues, including: (a) the role of local Afghan NGOs in rebuilding education; (b) the best way to focus services, that is, whether reaching the most rural and marginalized communities should be sacrificed for concentrating education programmes in more populous areas where government capacity and partnership opportunities were higher; and (c) how to design in a context of uncertain security.

The two NGO consortia that are the focus of this case study worked sequentially with virtually the same partners through most of the 2000s. They are: the Afghanistan Basic Education Consortium (ABEC), made up of CARE, CRS, the International Rescue Committee (IRC), Save the Children and the University of Massachusetts Center for International Education (CIE); and the Partnership for Advancing Community-Based Education in Afghanistan (PACE-A) made up of CARE, CRS, IRC and the Aga Khan Foundation (AKF).

Funded by the Asia Development Bank and in operation from 2004 to 2005, ABEC worked with the MoE and communities in eight provinces to improve basic education. ABEC partners committed to six strategies to improve school access and quality:

1. Community participation.
2. Reconstruction and construction of schools.
3. Supply of teaching and learning materials.

4. Training and support for quality teaching and learning in basic education.
5. Non-formal basic education activities such as early childhood development, accelerated learning and health education.
6. Management and monitoring of schools with participation of the MoE.

ABEC focused heavily on direct material and service provision, responding to immediate need while weighing community development and oversight more heavily than institutional development. ABEC supported both community-based schools and official government primary schools. ABEC partners prioritized delivering teaching and learning materials and ensuring that teachers were at least minimally qualified to teach. Also, no one could argue with building schools if there was money available to do it. Partners aligned the programme with existing (or evolving) government policies by using the national curriculum, ensuring that schools were constructed according to national guidelines, and with the MoE on project monitoring.

In 2006, PACE-A partners asserted in their proposal to USAID that the community-based education 'model developed during the height of Afghanistan's turbulent years is tough enough to weather the difficult years of reconstruction' (*PACE-A Response to RFA No. 306-06-004, 9*). In other words, a programme designed to work during the Taliban era should continue to be effective in the post-Taliban context of 'fragility'. The hardy model proposed small, quality schools responding to local needs for access and security that could integrate into the formal education system by becoming government-recognized schools. Early reconstruction-era (more relief-oriented) programmes like accelerated learning classes and literacy classes were proposed as a small component of the overall programme, but they were no longer meant to serve primarily as post-Taliban 'catch-up' schools, as they did in the initial relief and reconstruction phase. They were now positioned as training grounds for older girls who might then create a pool of relatively qualified female teachers, especially in remote areas, who would respond to local needs for access and security while integrating into the formal system.

PACE-A proposed five major objectives:

1 Expand access to community-based schools, particularly for girls and women, where MoE schools are not available.
2. Strengthen community structures and processes that support basic education.
3. Improve the quality of community-based education (CBE), particularly teaching.
4. Build the long-term capacity of Civil Society Organizations (CSOs) to support and sustain CBE.

5. Develop modes of cooperation between community-based and MoE schools and promote MoE recognition of and support for community-based education (*PACE-A Response to RFA No. 306-06-004*).

The PACE-A team drew on our institutional experience in working with communities, the MoE, local partners and each other. We worked to design the best possible intervention in light of our experiences in programming throughout the Taliban years and during the initial years of reconstruction. As the aid context moved slowly from relief to development, we were torn between long-term development by supporting the emerging Afghan state and doing right by Afghan children in the short-term, rather than years down the road. We were operating within a relief *and* a development context. Within a context of stabilization and increased government involvement, we optimistically designed for sustainability while planning for instability and weak capacity. We improved a hardy, tested model that could weather the insecurity and poor capacity we expected would remain entrenched by designing for incorporation into a MoE that was growing in reach and capacity.

Coordination with the Ministry of Education

Coordination with the state school system varied in the initial post-conflict years before and during the ABEC programme. Many providers, such as CARE and CRS, used the established national curriculum in their classrooms to ensure that student achievement and eventually schools might be officially certified, which would pave the way for MoE support, and in order to cooperate with the new regime. CRS accelerated learning classes were supervised by government schoolteachers, providing a link to the formal system as well as a feedback mechanism to bring the more active learning and participatory techniques used in accelerated learning classrooms into the formal schools through exposing monitors to the efficacy of the active learning approach. CARE and IRC worked to integrate students and teachers into the MoE system, frequently handing over entire schools to the MoE to become official government schools. At the same time, the relative chaos of the early reconstruction years resulted in numerous unregulated local innovations that responded to student need without necessarily coordinating with the formal system.

As the MoE grew in capacity by 2005, it took an increased interest in NGO education activities, including those of ABEC. An official evaluation of ABEC carried out by McNerney/CIE in 2005 noted that at the project's beginning, its small size and relative unimportance in comparison to larger policy issues meant that the MoE was generally uninvolved in project design or implementation (McNerney, 2005). However, management and policy changes during the life of the project led the MoE to become 'very active' at multiple levels, engaging more with donors and implementers to argue for uniformity of approach (ibid., 6). McNerney notes that 'this welcomed change does create problems however, given that the programme had already developed a series of working conditions and routines, which were difficult to adjust given the limited remaining time left in the project' (ibid., 6–7).

By project's end, ABEC partners concluded the following about working with the MoE:

- A central coordination unit greatly increased the ease of coordination with the MoE for each individual partner.
- It is crucial to engage with the MoE at multiple levels – at the district, provincial and national levels.
- Engaging with the MoE to monitor project activities provided an opportunity for district and provincial MoE staff to fulfil their desire to provide technical assistance. (*ABEC Continuation Concept Note, ABEC PCU*)

From the MoE perspective, ABEC's attempts to strengthen the MoE system could have been stronger. In his evaluation, McNerney reports that a department manager at the MoE 'wished that the NGOs would concentrate less on the numbers [of enrolled students, trained teachers and schools established] and more on creating sustainable projects that can be sustained by the ministry. Too many projects produce numbers, he said, but very few construct a system' (McNerney, 2005: 28).

In his evaluation, McNerney included comments from MoE officials that 'foreshadow the structure of future relations between NGOs and the ministry in Afghanistan' (ibid., 29). Addressing concerns about sustainability, area of operations, donor commitment and the role of local civil society and government, the MoE critique shows how 'aid' impacted education in the fragile state context. These comments, shared and discussed below, highlighted issues that International NGO (INGO) actors considered during the PACE-A programme design post-ABEC.

The majority of PACE-A partners had participated in ABEC, and we grappled with the MoE's insights and questions while designing PACE-A. Our development values challenged us to promote sustainability and develop local capacity, but our 'relief' mindset kept the most underserved Afghans at the top of our minds. We strove to strengthen the state education system and serve the most remote girls and boys while remaining cautious about security and state capacity. Community-based education offered a unique solution.

School construction

As ABEC concluded, partners agreed that reconstruction and rehabilitation activities were not their core capacity. CRS, for example, was challenged by school construction for multiple reasons: flooding in the remote locations chosen as construction sites delayed construction for months, necessitating transporting construction supplies by donkey; the division of a province into two new provinces meant working with an entirely new set of provincial officers halfway into construction; and an MoE request required relocation of a school site after significant community engagement had taken place in the initial location. School construction was thus significantly more expensive than budgets allowed. The MoE required a multi-classroom primary school design that cost roughly US$30,000 per school to construct, and, since school construction required close collaboration with the MoE, there was no possibility to build anything simpler and cheaper. The schools were designed to be large and solid, with high retaining walls to create secure playgrounds for children. Though we all accepted the MoE's jurisdiction to enact strict construction guidelines for high-quality schools, it was challenging to follow them, especially in remote locations. Moreover, building large schools was an exceedingly expensive strategy when trying to increase general access. As partners thought through next steps post-ABEC, we posited that the MoE could work directly with the growing private construction industry to build schools on their own. PACE-A partners chose to rely on existing structures – homes, mosques and the occasional community centre – to house community-based schools.

Teacher salaries and support

> I am very concerned about sustainability. Certainly it is good that the schools were built and that some teachers were trained, but I think that the teacher training part will not be supported after the [ABEC] project. Also good was the creation of community support through the village education committees and other community organizations. This additional support is good but I do not know how long it will last without outside support. (MoE official reflecting on ABEC in McNerney, 2005: 28)

The MoE official expressed the real and valid concern that donor support would dry up after the ABEC project ended, and that without external support, new systems would fail and new capacities would wither away. PACE-A partners agreed that donor support would eventually end, but we took the developmental approach and worried more about the long-term effects of creating dependency. Our strategy was to promote community and government support for community-based schools rather than donor support. During this post-conflict reconstruction phase, PACE-A partners were guided by the education needs of those left out of the growing formal education system. Our vision was to help expand the reach and capacity of the government by supporting a network of complementary low-cost community schools – linked to the ministry – that could reach the rural and marginalized communities.

PACE-A partners referred to the proposed project as a 'rapprochement' between the formal and CBE systems, affirming the vision of an MoE that takes eventual responsibility for providing quality education to all Afghan children (*PACE-A Response to RFA No. 306-06-004, 35*). To do this, we aimed to integrate the majority of community-based schools created in the five-year project into the MoE, a practice that CARE and IRC had developed over previous years. This goal led to a model in which NGO partners support teachers and schools through ongoing training, teaching materials and learning materials, but not salaries or classroom space. Teachers were to be supported through community contributions, in cash or in kind, with a medium-term goal of salary support from the MoE. PACE-A partners believed that the responsibility to pay teachers ultimately lies with the MoE and has held this challenging stance in an effort to not create a parallel education system within Afghanistan.

A few local NGOs who considered joining the PACE-A consortium decided against it because they believed it was only fair to pay teachers for their work. CARE and IRC, through experience, knew that most communities would support teachers, but this proved to be an ongoing debate within consortium member education departments. CRS staff, for example, wrestled with the idea of asking parents to pay for education when education was legally supposed to be free, and the idea of a contribution rather than a fee was not clear. The easy thing to do would have been to pay teachers, but this would have meant serving far fewer communities and letting the MoE off the hook. We believed it was their responsibility to pay. Over time, though, this continued to be a matter of debate and a challenge to implement; community-based education providers in Afghanistan, led by PACE-A, secured funding from the MoE to pay CBE teachers. Many, but not all, CBE teachers were eventually paid by the MoE.

The MoE official quoted above in 2005 felt that teacher training would fade away after ABEC. In fact, the MoE's Teacher Education Programme (TEP) was about to launch, and in an effort to promote the eventual integration of our schools, we also used TEP. Our PACE-A teacher trainers would become TEP master trainers so that all CBE teachers trained would be that much closer to serving as official MoE teachers. Over time, as policy was developed to bring CBE teachers on to the MoE payroll, TEP training became required for accreditation. The debate over this approach within the consortium was minimal, but there was some mourning that we could not be radically creative in our teacher training.

Capacity building of government officials and local NGOs

> NGOs should employ more Afghans from the Ministry in these projects for train-ing purposes. These 'seconded' people could work in both the NGO and the MoE by splitting their time. (MoE official reflecting on ABEC, in McNerney, 2005: 29)

By 2005, capacity at the MoE was improving. The MoE had revised and refined education policies, an information system was under development and the MoE was taking a more prominent leadership role when engaging with the donor community. Additionally, a few MoE leaders were inspir-ing and extremely competent, but overall, capacity was lacking. The offi-cial quoted above highlighted the strong need for training and support at the MoE. Although the PACE-A consortium never considered bringing sec-onded MoE staff into our NGOs, we deliberated about how to engage the MoE in a meaningful way. Building off of our ABEC experience, we designed a project management body that could coordinate with the MoE as well as provide an umbrella body for all CBE providers in Afghanistan. By bringing all the players together, we could ease the MoE's task of coordinating dozens of education service providers, and we could share innovations that improved quality with the MoE to improve national policies. This structure eventually contributed to the development of the MoE's Community-Based Education Policy, which recognized community-based education as a major contributor to Afghanistan's education system.

After one year of PACE-A implementation, we modified the programme to second implementing partner staff to Provincial Offices of Education to serve as Community-Based Education Provincial Liaison Officers. These officers helped provincial education staff roll out the new national CBE policy.

> I would like more Afghan NGOs as partners in the new project. The reason is that they could receive training. We are getting to the point in the development of

the country where Afghans should take over more responsibilities. (MoE official
reflecting on ABEC, in McNerney, 2005: 29)

The MoE official clearly states that, by 2005, the window for relief from international actors had passed, and we all agreed, in principle. We knew that
longer-term development requires building local capacity, and CSOs are a key
piece of that puzzle. We also believed that CSOs would be able to work in more
remote and insecure areas than INGOs. The debate over which and how many
local partners to involve was a rowdy one during the programme design phase.
We eventually committed to building the long-term capacity of CSOs to sustain CBE through supporting, expanding and improving existing CSO-run
CBE activities, using sub-awards, developing capacity of CSO partners and
providing opportunities for mutual learning and exchange among CBE providers. However, we were unable to name local NGOs as part of the proposal
(PACE-A Response to RFA No. 306-06-004).

We could not settle on specific CSOs to partner with for a few reasons.
First, a few of the larger, established CSOs wanted to continue paying teacher
salaries, which did not mesh with our strategy. Second, CARE, IRC, CRS and
AKF already complemented each other geographically, for the most part, and
established CSOs tended to operate in similar location. It was hard enough to
figure out which INGO would take the lead in provinces where two partners
were already working without bringing new groups into the mix. Third, we
had a clear strategy for integrating our schools into the MoE, and some of
us felt that adding another layer of implementation would make that more
difficult.

Our commitment to working with local CSOs shifted over time. After the
first year of implementation, PACE-A negotiated with USAID to shift funds
from CSO support activities to support the Provincial Liaison Officers and
other efforts to integrate community-based education into the MoE. This was
primarily a budget issue. Partners had only planned to bring CSOs into PACE-A
in the project's second year or later, so the CSO pool of funds had not yet been
touched. We seized an opportunity to work more closely with and build the
capacity of the MoE in the remaining years of implementation because we
understood that ultimate sustainability lay with the MoE. We felt that working
with CSOs was not as crucial as supporting the MoE's CBE efforts.

Several PACE-A partners did eventually work with CSOs in a few provinces, but not to the extent originally intended. We remained challenged by
finding CSOs that would not pay teacher salaries.

Site selection

> If the project was to go ahead, the selection of sites would have to be improved. It seems that the partners have spread themselves out too much and that the impact of this project as a model was lost. As it is the project did not have high visibility. There was nothing that could be shown as a model; it was just pieces. I would suggest that the partners concentrate in one district in a province and create something that was sustainable. They should make sure that each school that they built had all of the support services that they put in place in all these other areas. It really should not have been a project to put out numbers but it should have been a project to demonstrate quality. (MoE official reflecting on ABEC, in McNerney, 2005: 28)

Geography was a major question during PACE-A programme design. Most partners wanted to work where we were already working, where we had existing staff, existing relationships and knew the literal and figurative terrain. Membership in the PACE-A consortium was partially dictated by geographic coverage.

We hotly debated saturation versus spread. Partners who argued for saturation wanted to take advantage of operating efficiencies, create critical mass and increase chances for integrating CBE schools into the MoE system. The closer that CBE schools were to each other, the closer they were to existing MoE schools, and the easier they were to reach, the more likely they were to integrate. Partners who argued for spread wanted to serve Afghanistan's most remote communities and, because they were already working on or planning on working in such places, found operating efficiencies there.

By the end of the proposal development phase, we created a system that allowed partners to choose to work where we had been working, and we either saturated regions or spread out according to however densely people lived and how many mountains separated villages (though by the programme's second year saturation became official policy). We created three categories of community-based schools, reflecting the ease of potential integration into the official MoE system based on proximity to existing MoE schools, degree of remoteness and other disadvantages. Each category had different timelines for creation and eventual integration, which made official our intention to bring even extremely remote hamlets into the MoE system. They included:

- Category A classes could be integrated into the MoE system in the first 2–3 years of the project. These classes or schools were situated close to formal schools in places where the MoE was willing to absorb new classes by annexing the class, bringing CBE students to the formal school or clustering a group of CBE classes to make a new school. These classes often served girls in villages where boys already had access to school.

- Category B classes were targeted for integration into the MoE system in the fourth or fifth year of the project. These classes were located further away from a formal school than those classes in category A, and they may have served both girls and boys. Integration into the MoE system required MoE takeover of the entire school.
- Category C classes were not expected to integrate into the MoE system during the life of the project. They served extremely remote villages. Category C classes required additional mobilization, training and funding for post-project support until they could be absorbed by the MoE. While we did not expect to hand over these classes to the MoE during the project, we ensured that they were prepared for handover through thorough coordination with the MoE.

Uncertain security

Finally, PACE-A partners only worked in regions where we thought it would be safe to do so. Partners employed local staff to work in villages in regions they knew well. In some cases, married couples were hired so that women staff could travel to train and support village women and girls, a necessity in conservative rural areas. Partners were optimistic that security would hold in select areas of Afghanistan but designed PACE-A to be resilient in case the situation changed. The community-based education model was designed to remain sufficiently robust if partner or MoE staff were unable to visit due to security concerns. Local villagers taught at and monitored the school and could function without outsiders. As the programme continued, partners working in insecure areas relied heavily on local School Management Committees and nearby MoE school headmasters to monitor CBE schools and share feedback with NGO partners via telephone. Built into programme design was also the option to sub-grant to local CSOs, which were thought to be able to reach more insecure regions. This was done in only two provinces.

Even with these strategies in place, some PACE-A schools closed temporarily due to insecurity. Additionally, as aid workers increasingly became targets for attack, it became more and more difficult for the INGO staff to travel and visit schools. A devastating incident in 2008 where four IRC staff – a mix of Afghans and non-Afghans – were killed in an ambush led to restricted staff movement across many NGOs. Even though the attack was unrelated to PACE-A programming, the effects were felt within the project.

Despite these difficulties, the path we chose of designing for sustainability while planning for insecurity worked (Burde & Linden, forthcoming). As violence has increased across Afghanistan, it is the 'shiny new' government schools that are most often under attack within the education system. A report released in 2009 documented only one such attack on a community-based school pointing to the robustness of the model for both relief and development contexts (Glad, 2009). Some have argued that the difference in visibility and community support and involvement between government schools and community-based schools are some of the reasons for the stark distinction in attacks. It is indeed harder to attack a school if you do not know where it is, if it is blended seamlessly into the community fabric and, perhaps even more importantly, protected by the parents and community members invested in running it.

Conclusion
Zuki Karpinska

Humanitarian aid funding is usually short-term: for a period of months or approximately a year, perhaps two. This case study of a longer-term, that is, *five*-year, programme clearly illustrates the difficulties in planning for such a period in a situation of instability. Planners had to more-or-less predict the course of the conflict in Afghanistan and devise alternative methods of aid delivery for all of the conflict-phase variables. Planning for in-country humanitarian aid programmes and projects is often a 'shot in the dark'; proposals are written with footnoted contingency plans, with scores of project risks in the logical framework (a monitoring and evaluation tool typically used by aid agencies to track project progress and outcomes). The PACE-A planners seem to have hit the right balance of flexibility and caution.

The success of the programme was in no small way assisted by an innovative approach that placed much of the responsibility of programme implementation on communities committed to education. Groneman (2010) lists the community-based schooling approach as a prevention measure against attacks on education, which – in this instance – clearly worked.

Returning, however, to the main theme of this chapter, it is important to note that linkages between relief and development, since the 1990s, have become less of a focus than those between relief and security (Macrae & Harmer, 2004). Post-conflict, transition, rehabilitation or other such conceptual 'bridges' often take place in areas of resurgence of conflict and insecurity. Although many aid agencies engage in both humanitarian aid and development efforts, the former has a distinct set of principles that may not be congruent with development operations, such as neutrality (ibid.). There is, nevertheless, strong encouragement on the part of donors and other aid agencies for a continuous dialogue between the relief and development camps; often, both types of interventions are instituted at the same time. Coordination between these camps, as always, remains a challenge.

The IASC Early Recovery Cluster was established to address this 'gap' between humanitarian relief and development aid.

> Early recovery is a multidimensional process of recovery that begins in a humanitarian setting. It is guided by development principles that seek to build on humanitarian programmes and catalyze sustainable development opportunities. It aims to generate self sustaining, nationally owned, resilient processes for post crisis recovery. It encompasses the restoration of basic services, livelihoods, shelter, governance, security and rule of law, environment and social dimensions, including the reintegration of displaced populations. (Cluster Working Group on Early Recovery, 2008: 6)

It is a 'cross-cutting' sector, meaning that attention to early recovery should be part of all other humanitarian sector planning processes. Yet, the Early Recovery Cluster suffers from even lower levels of funding than the Education Cluster.

Finally, 'working in consortia' is one of the particularly interesting themes in this case study that is missing from the rest of the volume. Although partnerships have been described elsewhere, consortia are an altogether different arrangement, one that is preferred by donors investing large blocks of funding. A CARITAS contribution to a European Commission consultation states that, although working in consortia 'might not be a bad thing per se in terms of scaling up a given response and improv[ing] coordination', it privileges the larger NGOs that are likely to receive funding, anyway (CARITAS, 2011: 6). In this case study, building the capacity of the MoE took precedence over building the capacity of local CBOs given the nation-building aspects critical to this specific post-conflict setting. This decision reflects the assumption of the planners that – since governments are the duty-bearers of the right to education – their ability to provide services is crucial to recovery from crisis. Other planners may have reached a different decision, but – as the case studies in the volume demonstrate – programming decisions are made based on the information available and institutional strategies.

Key questions

- What are the challenges of programme planning in an unpredictable context in which levels of (in)security differ from month to month and village to village (i.e. in a relief *and* development context)?
- What are the advantages and disadvantages of community-based educational provision?
- How can conflicting institutional cultures, practices and favoured approaches of aid agencies working in consortia be managed?

Further reading

Cluster Working Group on Early Recovery. (2008), *Guidance Note on Early Recovery.* Geneva: UNDP, Bureau for Crisis Prevention & Recovery.

An introduction to the issues that should be considered in any externally funded humanitarian intervention, that is, issues crucial to planning for the eventual takeover of service delivery by governments.

Glad, M. (2009), *Knowledge on Fire: Attacks on education in Afghanistan. Risks and measures for successful mitigation.* Atlanta, GA: CARE. Retrieved 31 July 2011 from http://www.care.org/newsroom/articles/2009/11/Knowledge_on_Fire_Report.pdf.

An excellent report of the issues related to the protection of education from attack, including the nature of attacks and prevention measures.

Macrae, J. and Harmer, A. (2004), 'Beyond the continuum: An overview of the changing role of aid policy in protracted crises', in A. Harmer and J. Macrae (eds), *Beyond the Continuum: The changing role of aid policy in protracted crises.* HPG Report 18. London: ODI.

An examination of the different strategies, funding mechanisms and cooperation approaches used by traditional development actors and humanitarian aid agencies in situations of protracted crisis.

References

Buchanan-Smith, M. and Maxwell, S. (1994), 'Linking relief and development – an introduction and overview'. *IDS Bulletin 25*(4), 1–18.

Burde, D. and Linden, L. (forthcoming), *The Effects of Proximity on School Enrollment: Evidence from a randomized controlled trial in afghanistan.* Working Paper, Steinhardt School of Culture, Education, and Human Development, New York University.

Caritas Europa. (2011), *Response to the EU Public Consultation 'What funding for EU External Action beyond 2013?'* Brussels: Caritas Europa. Retrieved 31 July 2011 from http://www.caritas-europa.org/module/FileLib/CaritasEuropaResponse_PublicConsultationonEUExternalActionFunding.pdf.

Cluster Working Group on Early Recovery. (2008), *Guidance Note on Early Recovery.* Geneva: UNDP, Bureau for Crisis Prevention & Recovery.

Glad, M. (2009), *Knowledge on Fire: Attacks on education in Afghanistan. Risks and measures for successful mitigation.* Atlanta, GA: CARE. Retrieved 31 July 2011 from http://www.care.org/newsroom/articles/2009/11/Knowledge_on_Fire_Report.pdf.

Groneman, C. (2010), 'Desk study on field-based mechanisms for protecting education from targeted attack', in UNESCO (ed.), *Protecting Education from Attack: A state-of-the-art review.* Paris: UNESCO.

Macrae, J. and Harmer, A. (2004), 'Beyond the Continuum: an overview of the changing role of aid policy in protracted crises', in A. Harmer and J. Macrae (eds), *Beyond the Continuum: The changing role of aid policy in protracted crises.* HPG Report 18. London: ODI.

McNermey, F. (2005), *Final Evaluation: ABEC Afghanistan.* Amherst: Center for International Education, University of Massachussetts.

Maxwell, D., Webb, P., Coates, J. and Wirth, J. (2008), *Rethinking Food Security in Humanitarian Response.* Paper Presented to the Food Security Forum; 16–18 April 2008, Rome.

Thevenaz, C. and Resodihardjo, S. L. (2010), 'All the best laid plans . . . conditions impeding proper emergency response'. *International Journal of Production Economics 126,* 7–21.

Crisis Prevention: DRR through Schools in India

Debdutt Panda and John Abuya

Chapter Outline

Introduction   130
Case study   131
  Background to ActionAid's work on DRR   132
  Case context   135
  Partnership   136
  Embedding DRR in the community   138
  Advocacy   140
  Integration of DRR into curricula   141
  Analysis   143
Conclusion   143

Introduction

Zuki Karpinska

The bulk of humanitarian assistance is concentrated in only a handful of recipient countries. In 2008, the top ten humanitarian aid recipient countries accounted for almost two-thirds of humanitarian aid assistance (GHA, 2010). The majority of these countries are classified as complex emergencies, or humanitarian crises resulting from chronic or intermittent conflict. Sudden onset natural disasters, such as the tsunami of 2004 or the Haiti earthquake of 2010, also attract a significant portion of available funding. As seen in Chapter 3, the decision to allocate funding to a particular crisis may be based on donor country interests in statebuilding or preserving peace in a given region, as well as protecting donor country investments in the area.

Humanitarian funding is – for the most part – reactive: funding is allocated after the impacts of a crisis are known, despite growing recognition that the gravity of a particular crisis may be mitigated by preventative measures designed to minimize vulnerability. Worldwide, approximately 1.2 billion students are enrolled in primary and secondary schools; of these, 875 million school children live in high seismic risk zones and hundreds of millions more face regular flood, landslide, extreme wind and fire hazards (INEE et al., 2010). There are areas of the world where natural disasters occur cyclically, and not enough funding is allocated to prepare for crises that are predictable.

Although some cost-benefit analyses have proven the adage that 'an ounce of prevention is worth a pound of cure', it is morally repugnant to place a monetary value on human life; yet, crisis prevention measures can and do save lives. Conflict mitigation strategies – such as peace education – and disaster risk reduction (DRR) strategies – such as early warning systems – are often separate considerations in the practice of humanitarian aid.[1] This chapter highlights one of these – DRR – to show how aid agencies are using education to prevent and/or mitigate crisis.

DRR is 'generally understood to mean the broad development and application of policies, strategies and practices to minimize vulnerabilities and disaster risks throughout society' (Twigg, 2009: 8). It is the 'conceptual framework of elements considered [. . .] to avoid (prevention) or to limit (mitigation and preparedness) the adverse impacts of hazards, within the broad context of sustainable development' (ISDR, 2004: 17).

In 2005, the UN International Strategy for Disaster Reduction (ISDR) served as the secretariat for an agenda set by the World Conference on Disaster Risk Reduction in Kobe, Japan. The resulting document, *The Hyogo Framework for Action 2005–2015: Building the Resilience of Nations and Communities to Disasters* (HFA), was adopted by 168 countries. Of particular importance to the field of education is HFA priority 3 – 'use knowledge, innovation and education to build a culture of safety and resilience at all levels' – and its associated key activities: (a) information management and exchange, (b) education and training, (c) research and (d) public awareness (ISDR, 2005).

This case study presents the DRR work of ActionAid International in India and the reception of ActionAid activities by the crisis-prone communities who participated in the project. The case study also looks at the reception of DRR interventions by government officials, as government support of crisis prevention measures is integral to their success.

Case study
Debdutt Panda and John Abuya

Background to ActionAid's work on DRR

In line with ActionAid's vision – *a world without poverty and injustice in which every person enjoys their right to a life of dignity* – the organization works with poor and excluded people to eradicate poverty and injustice in approximately fifty countries. Using a Human Rights Based Approach (see Chapter 1), ActionAid's Global Strategy 2005–10 identified six thematic areas for focus, namely: women's rights; food rights; right to just and democratic governance; right to education; right to a life of dignity in the face of HIV/AIDS; and the right to human security in emergencies and conflict.

ActionAid's DRR work falls under the Right to Human Security in Emergencies and Conflict thematic area, and recognizes that there is an interdependent relationship between poverty and vulnerability, whereby the likelihood of denial of people's rights is greater in times of disasters for those who are already living in poverty.

A central pillar of ActionAid's DRR work, Disaster Risk Reduction through Schools (DRRS) Project was conceptualized in 2005 along with ActionAid's *Rights to End Poverty* Global Strategy. The DRRS Project was a joint concept by the Human Security and Education thematic areas, which led the DRRS Project design, consultations and buy-in as part of the global strategy development process. DRR interventions were to be implemented *through* schools not just *in* schools, recognizing the catalytic potential for change through education. The rationale behind the adopted methodology is that a school can be a locus for change: not only for increasing institutional capacity to strengthen resilience, but also for mobilizing communities to deliver an authentic DRR message consistent with local needs. The DRRS Project design aimed to bring together rights holders – particularly the poor and the marginalized – and the duty-bearers – those who are responsible for ensuring that the rights are upheld – at local, regional and national levels.

The purpose of the project was thus twofold: to make schools in high-risk disaster areas safer; as well as to enable them to act as a locus for disaster risk reduction, institutionalizing implementation of the HFA within education systems.

When the project began, it was sketched only in broad lines. The overall goal was clear: to reduce people's vulnerability to disasters related to natural hazards by contributing towards the implementation of the HFA. But, back in

2005, the HFA had only just seen the light of the day. Awareness of DRR and climate change were far less widespread than they are today.

ActionAid had a tested approach for working on vulnerabilities: Participatory Vulnerability Analysis (PVA). PVA is a tool used by ActionAid for building awareness and understanding of why disasters occur and how they can be reduced. The process involves a joint analysis – including vulnerable communities, local leaders and government officials – of hazards and their aggravating factors, highlighting community strengths in the process and discussing potential solutions for reducing risks. This shared analysis helps assign roles and responsibilities to different actors so that, in the event of a disaster, communities can hold these actors to account. The PVA approach was, however, still relatively little known in some of the countries that engaged with the project. ActionAid had had extensive experience of participation and mobilization of communities, and of work around the human security theme. However, overall, the DRRS Project demanded that ActionAid and its partners tackle a relatively new subject and do so in novel ways. Through the PVA process, it became clear that natural disasters are not the only risks or threats communities face, but rather that communities face a host of economic, political, social and/or cultural threats. These analyses, and especially the link to poverty, informed the general approach of ActionAid's DRR work and helped to justify its inclusion in the Global Strategy. It became very clear that disasters are not natural, and that they link to social justice.

Disasters disproportionally affect the poor. The poorest people, precisely because they are poor, are also the most exposed to the effects of disasters. They frequently do not have the means to defend themselves or the choice to move away from threats. In a vicious circle, because they are affected by disasters, they are kept in a poverty trap. DRR had to be looked at through the perspective of social justice as a possible key to breaking the cycle that maintains people in poverty. DRR initiatives were also to be built on the assumption that mitigating threats is often only one side of the coin. When tackling the root causes of vulnerability, DRR work should also address the socio-economic imbalances that make some people more vulnerable to crisis than others.

Climate change also disproportionally affects the most vulnerable. Many communities served by the DRRS Project are experiencing changes in seasonal patterns, in rainfalls, in the strength of recurring hazards. Their livelihoods are affected, and their traditional coping mechanisms need to be transformed. Through a social justice perspective, the costs and repercussions of climate change on poor communities needed to be acknowledged. This must lead state and international bodies to establish fair and equitable policies to address these challenges. The DRRS Project had joined forces with other organizations and networks in working on climate change issues, to bring into international fora the voices and experiences of the most vulnerable.

It is important to note that natural disaster, not just conflict, is also overwhelmingly 'man-made'. Human activities have a role in causing disasters, but the costs and benefits of such activities are not equally spread. Vulnerability analysis conducted through the DRRS Project started to highlight that 'development' work – whose benefits had not been felt in vulnerable communities – had nevertheless contributed to their vulnerability. In its short life-span, the DRRS Project did not adequately engage in mobilizing communities to demand redress for the negative externalities of development initiatives. But such issues are now on the table, and communities, partner NGOs and ActionAid itself are considering how best to tackle them.

The emphasis of the DRRS Project was on developing innovative solutions to vulnerability. The seven countries implementing the project were given a free hand to try and test approaches. The project was designed with a strong emphasis on learning: *an effective methodology will be developed that can be replicated in other schools, influencing national level policy and practice in ways that can be easily replicated in other countries and other sectors.* Support for peer review opportunities were thus built into the project proposal.

The theory behind the project's conceptualization and design suggested that the benefits of promoting DRR through schools would include:

- Building on the position of schools as the heart of predominantly rural communities, which are often surrounded by weak civil society structures and public services, and thus providing the opportunity to build physical and social capital.
- Harnessing space to promote learning and understanding, as schools are fora for developing knowledge among pupils and their teachers, and promoting child-to-child learning and child-to-parent learning to maximize DRR knowledge circulation.
- Creating a power base to mobilize the wider community, particularly through supporting school children to serve as important agents of change, as providing DRR knowledge to students results in the speedy dissemination of that information to parents and guardians, who in turn circulate it throughout the community.
- Strengthening educational networks of civil society actors – which may include teachers unions as well as other coalitions and community-based organizations (CBOs) – and promoting collaboration within and among these networks, ActionAid partners and governments from the community level to the national level in order to bring about structural change, for instance in education policy and curricula.
- Facilitation of a wider agenda for change, that is, broad dissemination of DRR messages using multiple actors such as NGOs and CBOs at the local level; and government bodies, UN agencies, the private sector and academia at the national

level; as well as lobbying international institutions like the UN/ISDR, UNESCO and UNICEF at the international level for greater focus on these issues.

The theory underpinning the DRRS Project was consistent with the prevailing international agenda on DRR. Indeed, ActionAid has been a major contributor to the development and promotion of the HFA since its inception in 2005. In preparation for the Kobe conference, ActionAid developed a paper titled 'Essential Ingredients for Successful People-Centred Early Warning Systems' and lobbied, along with others, for the Framework's adoption. More recently, the 2006–07 UN/ISDR campaign 'Disaster Risk Reduction Begins at School' aimed to promote the integration of DRR into government plans for school curricula and to ensure that school buildings are safe from the impacts of natural hazards. The current International Decade of Education for Sustainable Development led by UNESCO provides a long-term focus for taking this agenda forward. The DRRS Project was therefore seen as complementary and highly relevant to this broader international agenda, which continues to be committed to education as a catalyst for achieving sustainable progress as part of the broader DRR effort.

Strategically, ActionAid's commitment has been to address DRR imperatives, as espoused by the HFA, through targeted resources to country programmes identified to be in acute need of DRR support. The DRRS Project has been implemented in nine countries – Bangladesh, Ghana, Haiti, India, Kenya, Malawi, the Democratic Republic of Congo, Zambia and Nepal – all of which are highly vulnerable to disasters, both in economic terms and in terms of potential mortality. This case study presents ActionAid's experience of project implementation in the state of Assam, India.

Case context

Assam is the second largest of the eight north-eastern states in India. Traditionally already a land of high rainfall, the state has now begun to experience the negative impacts of climate change. In 2009, uneven rainfall and record high temperatures caused a drought-like situation. With more than 70 per cent of the population dependent on agriculture, the drought had a serious impact on livelihood in the state.

Almost 45 per cent of Assam's total area is prone to floods, the major cause being the river Brahmaputra that runs through the state and is connected by over 30 major tributaries. Severe floods have occurred regularly since 1950, with significant flooding experienced every year in the 1990s and on several occasions since 2000. The most serious recent floods occurred in 2004, which affected 5.6 million people and killed 52. Assam is also located in a very high seismic zone, rendering the state vulnerable to earthquakes. Although the last major earthquake in the state occurred in 1950, this had a devastating impact on the state and its population needs to be prepared for any future earthquakes.

In addition to these natural hazards, Assam is also prone to the traditional man-made disaster of conflict; the state has experienced a high degree of political unrest since the 1970s. This stems from tension between the Assamese and Bengali populations, as well as a number of insurgent groups with separatist aspirations, and the conflict has resulted in widespread displacement. Since 2000, the situation has been relatively calm in the state, although the population remains acutely aware that problems could arise again at any time.

Around 95 per cent of the Nalbari district in Assam is flood-affected. Nalbari has also been particularly affected by political unrest over the past forty years. Many parts of the district remain underdeveloped: there is a serious lack of livelihood options in the district, with agriculture and a very limited number of government jobs being the only real employment opportunities for the local population. Disasters have caused a shift in livelihood towards daily wage labour, increasing the vulnerability of communities. The district also has a large Scheduled Tribe population, constituting 17.63 per cent of the total population. According to the 2001 Census, less than half of the villages in the district have a paved approach road, rendering them particularly vulnerable and difficult to access during floods; further, many villages lack electricity.

Partnership

ActionAid India's partner in Assam is Gramya Vikas Mancha[2] (GVM), a community-based organization with its headquarters in the Nalbari district. ActionAid began working with GVM during the floods of 2004, and was immediately impressed by their approach to disaster work. Characterized by a lack of hierarchy, GVM is a voluntary organization that emphasizes strong partnerships with beneficiary communities. As each village in which GVM works identifies volunteers who become part of the GVM team and their larger network, GVM manages to fully integrate into the communities in which it operates. GVM was, therefore, a natural partner for ActionAid's roll-out of the DRRS in Assam.

The project began with pilot PVA exercises in two villages: one PVA carried out at the school level in order to identify specific risks to the school infrastructure, and the other at the village/community level. The tools of analysis varied by context: in some, for example, maps were drawn of the village to identify low-lying areas at risk of flooding. Following this pilot phase, the PVAs were then carried out across the remaining participating villages to identify potential disaster risks and vulnerabilities.

The shift in the PVA findings over the course of three years demonstrates the evolution of the project. At the beginning of the project, villages primarily identified infrastructure needs as part of their individual disaster risk reduction strategies. As a result, the villages asked ActionAid and GVM to provide funding for core infrastructure work. Some of these infrastructure projects were supported by ActionAid and GVM through the DRRS Project. At one school, for example, the project provided the village funding to supply electricity to the school compound; at the same school, the project funded the raising of school land as it was previously low-lying and prone to flooding, so that the school would no longer have to close during heavy rains. However, over the course of the project, villagers asked the partner organizations to provide advocacy training in order to learn how to approach relevant government offices with their demands. For example, in a workshop carried out for people with disabilities, participants showed ActionAid their disability cards and asked workshop facilitators how to go about obtaining entitlements from the government. In fact, in the majority of villages, communities received training on the applicable assistance schemes that were already available in the country and on how to approach the authorities with requests.

Box 7.1 Advocacy work in Niruma Latima village with PVA findings

Niruma Latima village is located off a mud road in a remote area of Nalbari district. About 400 families live in the village, dependent on agriculture and fishing. GVM volunteers related that before the PVA approach was introduced, villagers were unable to articulate their needs and concerns to government officials who could help them. The PVA process identified and documented village issues such as lack of clean water, road access and electricity. Through the project's PVA processes, villagers were able to learn how to present written accounts of the issues they faced to government authorities. A list of names of below-poverty-line (BPL) families without electricity were passed on to the Electricity Board for action. The issue of a road connection was taken up with the Mahatma Gandhi National Rural Employment Guarantee Act (MGNREGA) authorities, who are responsible for an Indian job guarantee scheme. The NREGA programme provides for one hundred days of employment in every financial year to adult members of any rural household willing to do public-work-related unskilled manual labour – such as road construction – at minimum wage.

Finally, a canal blockage issue was resolved by building flood protection structures with the support of available government schemes. Since the first PVA was carried out in 2007, a number of problems identified by the villagers have already been addressed.

Box 7.2 Using the PVA to mobilize money from Sarva Shiksha Abhiyan (SSA)

Sarva Shiksha Abhiyan (SSA) is the Government of India's flagship programme for achievement of universal primary education. The programme seeks to open new schools in areas that do not have schooling facilities as well as to strengthen existing school infrastructure through provision of additional classrooms, toilets, drinking water, maintenance grants and school improvement grants. As part of the programme, existing schools with an insufficient cadre of teachers are provided with additional teaching staff. Teachers are also provided extensive training, grants for developing teaching-and-learning materials and a strengthened academic support structure at cluster, block and district levels.

Anchulik ME School, in Barbulik, has 90 students studying at the upper-primary level and 130 at the lower-primary level. In 2007, at the start of the DRRS Project, the school was constructed with bamboo. The first PVA, carried out in May 2007, identified this lack of permanent infrastructure as the major problem. Based on these findings, GVM and ActionAid invited the SSA authorities to visit the school and hold a public meeting. The SSA accepted the need for a proper school structure and sanctioned the building of one classroom in 2008. However, this room was not large enough to accommodate all the students, so the SSA were invited back to the village. The SSA representatives assessed the number of students attending the school and sanctioned two more classrooms in 2009.

Embedding DRR in the community

Critical to the success of the DRRS Project in Assam has been the active participation of a range of stakeholders and the partnerships developed. The advantage of working with GVM as an implementing partner is its integration into the community. Key to the GVM philosophy is that the organization does not introduce anything new: instead, GVM and its network of volunteers aims to strengthen and build upon existing community knowledge, capacities and coping mechanisms. Even before the DRRS Project, there were traditional methods for early warning prior to disasters, such as using drumbeats as an alert signal. Although the communities already had some mechanisms for disaster mitigation in place, they recognized that the pattern of disasters is changing and that these traditional systems were breaking down.

All of the villages selected as part of the DRRS Project were keen to participate because they are all seriously affected by floods on a regular basis; therefore, they could easily appreciate the value of DRRS work. GVM built up a large network of 3,000 volunteers – of which approximately 40 per cent were women – to implement and further develop the DRRS Project. This network of village-based volunteers was key to the success and sustainability of the work, as the volunteers are personally involved and motivated to continue DRR activities in their areas. The capacity of volunteers grew as the project progressed, as they received additional training and support from GVM and ActionAid. This enabled them to take on greater responsibility and leadership for DRR activities in their village.

Another key aspect of success was the use of resource teachers in the project, a project component that identified teachers to coordinate DRR activities in their schools and provide a crucial link between the school and the wider community. This element was introduced in 2008, in the second year of the project, when ActionAid and GVM realized that there had not been enough effort to involve the teachers in the original project design. The teachers in the catchment area are generally from the villages themselves, and rarely transfer to other schools. To overcome their initial hesitancy at adding to their work burden, GVM and ActionAid organized an orientation programme, to help teachers develop a better understanding of the importance of DRR work. The two partner organizations then conducted an exposure programme, through which the resource teachers were taken to different villages to see the various DRR activities that were in place, such as raised platforms and canal dredging. After this, the level of involvement of the teachers increased dramatically. Resource teachers work together as a network and meet every two months.

Halidhar Kalida, a resource teacher from Barbhag Kalig High School, explained the importance of the project to his community in the following words: 'This is a flood-prone area, and there are also risks of bomb blasts and earthquakes, yet we have a lack of human and financial resources to deal with them. This project has helped to develop resources and knowledge to benefit society.' He and other resource teachers have, through their participation in the project, gained the skills to take on their own advocacy work.

The involvement of children has also been crucial in the project, with a high degree of children's participation and children's initiatives being witnessed across all DRRS activities. Hazard Safety Cadet Corps (HSCC) and Community Life Guards (CLG) have been established in a number of villages. The HSCC and CLG carry out regular mock drills and training sessions, covering topics such as first aid and search and rescue; the HSCC now participates in the annual district-level mock drills. In addition, CLG units are trained to rescue people from flood situations. These activities have enabled a large group of youths to emerge as DRR change-makers in the project area.

A Children's Assembly has been established in four of the participating villages. This has provided the space for children to work together on DRR-related activities and to share learning through activities such as folksongs, plays and traditional games. Initially, these assemblies were organized at schools. However, GVM volunteers noticed that a significant number of children were missing out on this experience as they were attending private schools; consequently, assemblies have been extended to the village level and activities take place in the afternoon to allow the inclusion of all children from the village.

A crucial goal of the DRRS Project was to empower communities and to increase their resilience to deal with disasters. Community confidence in their capacity to cope with emergencies has increased dramatically over the life of the project. This confidence has resulted from the active involvement of various stakeholders in every aspect of the project, as well as from the first aid training and rescue techniques.

Advocacy

A key objective of the DRRS Project globally was to advocate for government adoption of the DRR agenda at a national level, implementation of the HFA that they have endorsed and incorporation of DRR into the school curriculum. One of the targets for the DRRS Project in India was to ensure that national-level policy and practice are influenced by local examples of excellence in DRR through schools.

Significant advocacy work has been carried out at the local, district and state levels in Assam. Some of this has been discussed above, in the way that PVAs and village-level action plans have been presented to government authorities and the work that has been sanctioned in response. Since the start of the project, GVM and ActionAid have been meeting regularly with panchayats, block-level authorities and district-level authorities to ensure their active engagement with and support of the project. For example, the organizations met repeatedly with the panchayat members to get them interested in the DRRS work and conducted an exposure programme to increase their level of understanding of DRR issues. As a consequence, all of them are now actively engaged in the project; further, it has helped with linking panchayat members to the community in terms of accessing funds for their Multi-Hazard DRR Action Plans.

Government authorities have, over the project period, recognized the importance of DRRS work and the team is now being used as a resource for district-level mock drills. In 2009, the HSCC participated in the district-level mock drill in Nalbari. GVM reported that they received excellent support from the Minister for Revenue and Disaster Management in Assam. This relationship has been facilitated by the fact that the whole area is flood-prone, so the authorities appreciate the importance and value of DRRS work. When a flood occurs, the government needs time to reach all the villages, so they appreciate the fact that GVM volunteers are already on-site, and they acknowledge the effective flood-relief work that GVM has been carrying out since 1999. Currently, DRR resource teachers are available only in schools participating in the DRRS Project. However, district authorities are aiming to expand the DRRS initiative across the whole district. Significant funds are required to reach all 1,600 schools, but a project officer from the District Disaster Management Authority explained that they are committed to finding the necessary funding for this expansion and that, once additional resources are available, the resource teachers' network will cover the entire district of Nalbari. GVM, along with current resource teachers, has recently submitted a request to the Inspector of Schools for the district calling for:

1. DRR resource teachers in all schools;
2. HSCCs to be established in all schools;
3. Participatory School Safety Audits to be carried out in all schools, leading to a School Multi-Hazard DRR Plan;
4. Mock drills to be carried out in all schools (at least twice a month);
5. School Disaster Management Committees to be established in all schools;
6. All schools to have an updated first aid box, including appropriate provisions for persons with disabilities.

Integration of DRR into curricula

One of the key goals of the DRRS Project in India was to promote pedagogical changes, so that DRR is incorporated into the school curriculum and all children can benefit from greater DRR knowledge and skills. Given the level of disaster risk in the state, children's understanding of risks and how to manage them should be reinforced through the curriculum, as well as through extra-curricular activities. It was understood that for this change to occur, long-term advocacy would be necessary. However, even in the three-year project period, progress towards this goal has been very successful. GVM and ActionAid held a number of district-level and state-level meetings and workshops to this end. A variety of stakeholders were also mobilized to advocate for DRR inclusion in the curriculum. For example, GVM and ActionAid have also managed to gain the support of the state-level Employees' Union (Karmachari Parishad) and the state-level Teachers' Union – both of whom have great influence on policy-makers – to integrate DRR issues in education programming. The organizations also worked closely with Dakshin Pub Nalbari Disaster Management Group, a group that comprises retired teachers, college principals, panchayat representatives and defence personnel. This group has been active in taking forward different disaster-related issues. From the start of the project, GVM and ActionAid have been holding regular discussions with government officials, in particular SSA representatives, regarding the inclusion of DRR in the school curriculum.

It has been decided that DRR will be included in the National Council of Education Research and Training (NCERT) – the premiere body of the Government of India in charge of developing school curricula and producing textbooks – state-level curriculum for social studies for classes 9 and 10 as of 2010. Although the textbooks are designed in Delhi, there is some scope for inclusion of locally relevant material, currently being developed by GVM and ActionAid. Monthly meetings with teachers from schools under the project have been held and teachers have also conducted field-testing of resource materials. An initial workshop was held in September 2009 to review existing textbooks and teaching-learning materials. The existing materials were then reviewed at a state-level workshop in November 2009, which included representatives from SSA, teachers and textbook writers. In this workshop, it was resolved that a separate textbook should be developed on DRR and climate change. However, until this textbook is developed, supplementary teaching-and-learning materials would be created as an interim measure. A follow-up state-level workshop took place in September 2010 to review the draft curriculum and to incorporate recent learning from the field, bringing together a number of government representatives, including those from SSA and the State Disaster Management.

Analysis

The success of the project has been acknowledged by participating communities, who recognized the value of crisis prevention measures and successfully lobbied government officials to take note. Advocacy work at the local, district and even state levels has been very fruitful during the three-year life span of the project. The adoption of PVA as a tool by authorities in the district demonstrates the effective working relationship that has been achieved between the GVM, ActionAid and government in the area. Some of the goals of the project were to influence the national agenda on DRR, implement the HFA and incorporate DRR into the school curriculum across the country. Although the project had a number of successes in terms of influencing the district- and state-level authorities regarding DRR, the national-level advocacy component was missing from the project. Given the project's great achievements in Assam, it would have been even more rewarding if the experience there could have been used to influence DRR developments at the national policy level.

The project's success was also acknowledged by a number of external actors. In particular, as the UK DFID-funded phase of the project approached completion, further funding was secured from the European Commission Humanitarian Aid department's Disaster Preparedness Programme (DIPECHO) to continue and develop DRR initiatives.

Conclusion
Zuki Karpinska

DRR – and education in general – are ongoing processes that are never completed; yet, focused attention and commitment to – as well as action for – crisis prevention may avert not only interruptions in the school cycle, but also loss of life. In this instance, education may clearly be seen as a potentially life-saving humanitarian response. This case study underscores the need for government commitment to crisis preparedness and prevention in order to effect the changes necessary to protect students and their communities. Much as service provision is the responsibility of governments, so is the protection of their citizenry from identified dangers in the face of often predictable – and sometimes preventable – crises.

There are 168 governments committed to the HFA. Governments world-over also committed to the MDGs and EFA targets. In 2010, the INEE co-led a consultative process to develop the *INEE Guidance Notes on Safer School Construction* with the Global Facility for Disaster Reduction and Recovery

(GFDRR) at the World Bank, and in partnership with: the Coalition for Global School Safety and Disaster Prevention Education, the IASC Education Cluster and the ISDR (INEE et al. 2010). These *Guidance Notes* provide a framework for guiding principles and general steps to develop a context-specific plan for disaster-resilient construction and retrofitting of school buildings. The *Guidance Notes* have in turn been recognized by the 2010 UN General Assembly Resolution on EiE (see Chapter 1):

> 11. *Also urges* Member States to ensure that disaster risk and safety considerations are factored into all phases of the planning, design, construction and reconstruction of educational facilities, through the consideration, inter alia, of the recommendations contained in the 'Minimum standards for education: preparedness, response, recovery' handbook of the Inter-Agency Network for Education in Emergencies and its 'Guidance notes on safer school construction.' (UNGA, 2010)

There are global pressures, therefore, to make crisis preparedness and prevention a routine and necessary component of humanitarian aid and education service provision. The ActionAid experience proves that – once communities are made aware of the possibilities of their own agency vis-à-vis government officials – local pressure to mainstream crisis prevention can also achieve attention to and action for this issue.

However, crisis prevention cannot be tackled as a set of isolated activities. There are clear linkages between poverty and vulnerability to disasters (Eriksen, 2007). The poorest segments of the population are hit hardest by natural disasters, setting development projects back for years or decades (World Bank, 2006). Similarly, attacks on schools in conflict-affected areas prevent only a fraction of school-aged children from attending schools; the bulk of out-of-school children in that area do not access education opportunities due to poverty, which in itself is caused or exacerbated by conflict. Much as education is the key to progress for the remaining MDGs, poverty reduction (MDG 1) is crucial for crisis prevention.

Key questions

- What is the utility of evaluating crisis prevention programmes in terms of cost–benefit ratios?
- What is the relationship among climate change adaptation, disaster risk reduction and conflict prevention?
- How can schools be effectively harnessed to disseminate life-saving messages?
- How can poverty reduction decrease crisis risk?

Notes

1   However, in a project concerned with the development and implementation of preventative measures in crisis-prone Gaza, UNESCO suggested expanding the term to include safety preparedness
measures during chronic conflict, coining it (c)DRR. Preliminary findings concerning the (c)DRR
project in the restricted areas of Gaza, UNESCO Office oPt. (n.d.), 'Safe Schools: Protecting education from attack'. Unpublished report.
2   Village Development Forum.

Further reading

Groneman, C. (2010), 'Desk study on field-based mechanisms for protecting education from targeted
attack', in UNESCO (ed.), *Protecting Education from Attack: A State-of-the-Art Review*. Paris:
UNESCO.

A presentation on the kinds of crisis prevention measures used to prevent attacks on education
in times of conflict and insecurity, including measures that address physical protection, provision
of alternative learning sites and schedules, negotiation of schools as conflict-free zones and
involvement of communities in the protection of education.

ISDR. (2005), *The Hyogo Framework for Action 2005–2015: Building the resilience of nations and
communities to disasters*. Extract from the final report of the World Conference on Disaster
Reduction (A/CONF.206/6). Retrieved 31 July 2011 from http://www.unisdr.org/eng/hfa/docs/
Hyogo-framework-for-action-english.pdf.

The fundamental global aid framework for disaster risk reduction, adopted by 168 states.

ISDR. (2007), *Towards a Culture of Prevention: Disaster risk reduction begins at school. Good practices
and lessons learned*. Geneva: ISDR.

A collection of case studies from around the globe on raising awareness for DRR, building a culture
of disaster prevention and making school buildings safer.

References

Eriksen, S. E. H., Klein, R. J. T., Ulsrud, K., Næss, L. O. and O'Brien, K. (2007), *Climate Change
Adaptation and Poverty Reduction: Key interactions and critical measures*. GECHS Report 2007:1.
Report prepared for the Norwegian Agency for Development Cooperation (Norad). Oslo, Norway:
GECHS International Project Office.

Global Humanitarian Assistance and Development Initiative. (2010), *GHA Report 2010*. Retrieved 31
July 2011 from http://www.globalhumanitarianassistance.org/report/gha-report-2010.

Groneman, C. (2010), 'Desk study on field-based mechanisms for protecting education from targeted
attack', in UNESCO (ed.), *Protecting Education from Attack: A state-of-the-art review*. Paris:
UNESCO.

INEE and GFDRR in partnership with the Coalition for Global School Safety and Disaster Prevention Education, the IASC Education Cluster and ISDRR. (2010), *Guidance Notes for Safer School Construction*. Retrieved 31 July 2011 from http://www.ineesite.org/assets/Guidance_Notes_Safer_School_Constructionfinal.pdf.

Twigg, J. (2009), *Characteristics of a Disaster-Resilient Community: A guidance note. Version 2.* London: DFID Disaster Risk Reduction Interagency Coordination Group. Retrieved 31 July 2011 from http://www.abuhrc.org/Publications/CDRC%20v2%20final.pdf.

UN General Assembly. (2010), *The right to education in emergency situations. A/64/L.58.* 30 June 2010.

UN International Strategy for Disaster Reduction (ISDR) (2004), *Living With Risk: A global review of disaster reduction initiatives.* Geneva: ISDR.

— (2005), *The Hyogo Framework for Action 2005–2015: Building the resilience of nations and communities to disasters.* Extract from the final report of the World Conference on Disaster Reduction (A/CONF.206/6). Retrieved 31 July 2011 from http://www.unisdr.org/eng/hfa/docs/Hyogo-framework-for-action-english.pdf.

— (2007), *Towards a Culture of Prevention: Disaster risk reduction begins at school. Good practices and lessons learned.* Geneva: ISDR.

UNESCO Office oPt (n.d.), *Safe Schools: Protecting education from attack.* Unpublished report.

World Bank Independent Evaluation Group. (2006), *Hazards of Nature, Risks to Development: An IEG evaluation of World Bank assistance for natural disasters.* Washington, DC: World Bank.

Cross-Cutting Issues: Youth-Centred Programming for Palestinian Refugees in Lebanon

8

Adona El-Murr

Chapter Outline

Introduction	147
Case study	149
Background	149
Context	149
Context analysis	150
Project development	152
Addendum	158
Conclusion	159

Introduction
Zuki Karpinska

In addition to the plethora of concerns that are already understood in the term 'education in emergencies' (see Chapter 1), a number of cross-cutting issues or themes are also to be considered. Cross-cutting implies that particular issues are common to a range of projects and programmes, and attention to these highlighted issues should be institutionalized (see Chapter 2) within programmatic strategies, planning processes and operations, as well as translated into action.

The lists of cross-cutting issues vary from actor to actor, from one humanitarian aid sector to another. The 2005 European Consensus on Development, a policy statement guiding the European Community's development vision and principles, lists the following cross-cutting issues: promotion of human rights, gender equality, democracy, good governance, children's rights and those of indigenous peoples, environmental sustainability and combating HIV/AIDS. The 2011 edition of the *Sphere Project Handbook* (see Chapter 2) considers cross-cutting themes to be children, older people, persons with disabilities, gender, psychosocial issues, HIV/AIDS, environment and climate change and disaster risk reduction. The 2010 edition of the *INEE Minimum Standards* (see Chapter 2) lists conflict mitigation, disaster risk reduction, early childhood development, gender, HIV/AIDS, human rights, inclusive education, inter-sectoral linkages, protection, psychosocial support and youth. The IASC requires that all clusters (see Chapter 5) focus on the following four cross-cutting issues: gender, age, environment and HIV/AIDS. Logically, if an issue were cross-cutting, it would be consistent across all of this guidance, as is gender. In practice, however, global humanitarian aid sector coordination bodies, international agencies, country programmes of individual agencies and country-level aid sector coordination groups each decide on the issues perceived to be most relevant to their programmatic needs and label these cross-cutting.

Yet, some of the issues considered cross-cutting cannot be reasonably addressed in all humanitarian aid programmes. The cross-cutting issues related to age in the abovementioned documents, for instance, sometimes single out youth, elderly and early childhood populations. Often, humanitarian aid programmes focus on a particular group of beneficiaries – such as primary-school aged children. In these cases, older persons and even early childhood development would not feature in programmatic considerations; thus, concerns related to these two themes cannot be taken up within (most) primary education programmes, despite institutional requirements to embed selected cross-cutting issues across all programming.

This chapter presents a case study of a project focused on one EiE cross-cutting issue: youth. The term 'youth' generally captures those between 15 and 24 years of age; yet, different sociocultural understandings of the term may increase this age span to even age 40. This case study examines how joint stakeholder analysis of the specific situation of Palestinian refugees led to a project that identified needs that were not being addressed by aid agencies operating in Lebanon. This case study offers insight into how youth mobilization for community development can offer benefits far beyond the project participant group.

Case study

Adona El-Murr

Background

From April 2008 until September 2009, the Increasing Employment Capacity and Conflict Resolution Skills in the Palestinian Refugee Camps of El-Buss and Rashidieh Project (IECCRS) was implemented in the south of Lebanon. Funded by the British Embassy's Global Opportunities Fund and implemented through the National Association of Vocational Training and Social Services (NAVTSS) in partnership with the Women's Humanitarian Organization and El-Quds Youth Centre, this project aimed to build the knowledge and skills of a group of Palestinian youth to identify community problems and possible solutions, while meaningfully engaging with their community to implement these solutions. The project also aimed to increase the ability of youth to secure employment, allowing participants to prepare for their future. The project used a new model and approach to vocational training that emphasized youth leadership and participation in order to fill gaps in existing aid agency programming.

Context

The creation of the state of Israel and the ensuing Arab–Israeli War displaced large numbers of Palestinians. Established by the UN General Assembly in 1949, the UN Relief and Works Agency for Palestine Refugees (UNRWA) is a relief and human development agency that provides services and humanitarian assistance to over 4.3 million refugees living in the Gaza Strip, the West Bank, Jordan, Lebanon and Syria. The Palestinian refugee population is the most sizeable group of refugees in the world. UNRWA is by far the largest UN operation in the Middle East, with over 27,000 staff, almost all of whom are refugees themselves.

Lebanon contains many diverse communities of various religious, social and cultural backgrounds and has historically been one of the most heterogeneous states in the Middle East region. Its 1943 National Covenant stipulated that parliamentary seats were to be divided according to a 1932 national religious census and that Lebanon's president was to be a Maronite Christian, the prime minister a Sunni Muslim and the speaker of parliament a Shi'ite Muslim. This system allows for political representatives to avoid social fragmentation across sectarian lines and the political hierarchy (Saud, 1998). The 1989 Taif Agreement, in an effort to end the Lebanese Civil War that began in 1975, built on the National Covenant power-sharing agreement and allocated state power and resources through 'confessional' structures, a political system that divides parliamentary seats equally among Christian and Muslim religious groups.

Palestinians have arrived in Lebanon in large numbers as of 1948, with further displacement continuing since then due to sporadic conflict. While 425,000 Palestinian refugees are registered with UNRWA in Lebanon, a recent study conducted by the American University of Beirut (AUB) and UNRWA estimates that only 260,000 – 280,000 currently reside in the country (Chaaban et al., 2010: x). In addition to their limited political rights as 'foreigners', Palestinian refugees in Lebanon are restricted from enjoying many social and civil rights, denied possession and property rights, and limited access to employment opportunities and government public health, education and other social services. Despite a recent amendment to stringent Lebanese employment laws for refugees, the reform '. . . does not have any political effects because the Lebanese unanimously agree on the Palestinians right of return and reject naturalization' (ibid.).

For the Palestinian refugee population, therefore, many of the services that are usually provided by governments to their citizenry fall under the mandate of UNRWA. There are 46 Arab organizations and 20 external NGOs that offer assistance to Palestinian refugees in Lebanon (ibid.), but the majority of the Palestinian community relies entirely on UNRWA as the sole provider of education, healthcare, other social services and relief aid. In the Lebanon Field Office (LFO), UNRWA employs over 3,000 staff and provides services to registered refugees, who mainly reside in 12 camps and other settlements known as gatherings.

Context analysis

The IECCRS Project began with a joint brainstorm by aid workers, community leaders and other stakeholders on how youth-led community engagement could be a part of conflict transformation and community mobilization in times of political instability. The project organizers conducted a thorough context analysis that formed the basis of project planning. Addressing barriers to education and employment, as well as strengthening a culture of community engagement and empowerment, were identified as major needs within the community and gaps within the existing responses of development institutions.

Employment and education

Approximately 50 per cent of the Palestinian refugee population in Lebanon is below the age of 25 years (ibid.) The overall development of children and youth has been dramatically affected by the limited rights of Palestinian refugees in Lebanon, as well as by latent and overt conflict.

UNRWA schools in Lebanon face overcrowding in addition to other challenges, with most UNRWA schools on a double shift. There is a high rate of discontinuation from elementary to intermediate to secondary education. Youth are interested in pursuing their education beyond an intermediate level, but opportunities do not match demand. Only 13 per cent of Palestinian refugees complete secondary school education and post-secondary education (ibid., xi). The UNRWA Mid-Term Plan 2005–09[1] acknowledged that existing vocational training programmes were deemed outdated, poorly linked to the labour market, and under-resourced. Refugee women, in particular, tend to leave the education system early and do not enter the work force.

Considered 'foreigners', Palestine refugees face challenges in gaining lawful employment with an estimated 56 per cent of refugees jobless between the age of 23 and 65 years (ibid.). This has prevented a large proportion of refugees from ensuring sustainable livelihoods for themselves and their families, pushing them further into poverty. The majority of Palestinian refugees in Lebanon live below the poverty line: the poorest 20 per cent of the population lives on US$72 per person per month, and the richest 20 per cent lives on US$325 per person per month (Chaaban et al., 2010: 28).

Social networks

Palestinian refugees use social networks to increase individual access to the limited service infrastructure that is available to them. The networks, however, often exclude the elderly as well as female-headed, mobile and poor households; these households thus experience lower labour force participation and education levels, as well as poorer health, than the population that has access to the networks (FAFO, 2003).

Young people who do not study or work are among the most marginalized youth, but also the most hard-to-reach because they do not have access to formal networks within the labour market nor to educational systems. Young women have even fewer opportunities than young men. Children and youth attempt to overcome the difficulties of their circumstances through family support and solidarity, early marriage, finding belonging and acceptance within their camp community, avoiding tense social settings, peer support, religion, Palestinian identity, education, political activism and youth groups.

Youth programmes

Children-and-youth activities are carried out by grassroots organizations with direct access to communities; these organizations comprise the few facilitators of social, cultural, art and sports activities.[2] The clubs and centres lack technical and resource support, especially for improving the physical infrastructure and obtaining the equipment necessary to lead activities. In addition, many of the available youth clubs are, or are perceived to be, affiliated with various Palestinian political parties, increasing the complexities of aid organizations that wish to maintain neutrality and avoid being branded as partial to any particular party.

These NGOs, clubs and centres often do not have a long-term vision, strategies, or policies for their work with youth beyond their immediate activities. The NGOs tend to undertake only rudimentary impact assessments of their work; as a result, there is little basis for innovation in youth activities, compounded by the fact that the NGOs have similar donors who support similar types of activities.

UNRWA's work with children and youth has typically consisted of distinct projects within its programming in education, healthcare, relief, other social service provision, infrastructure development and emergency aid.

Challenges for UNRWA in the sector of children and youth include the coordination and sharing of information available on children and youth, capacity building for UNRWA staff and partner organizations working with children and youth, and meaningful engagement with communities to establish programming priorities that address children and youth as a cross-cutting theme. This is consistent with gaps identified across the organizations working with young adult refugees in Lebanon: youth programming requires innovation, commitment and participation of partner organizations and stronger linkages across the sector. Notably, there has been significant improvement in UNRWA-LFO youth services since 2008.

Project development

The IECCRS Project was developed and driven by local and international aid workers who had been working with various NGOs and agencies delivering services to Palestinian refugees in Lebanon. Upon forming an independent group, they were not bound by the conventions and bureaucratic processes of these organizations and thus had more latitude in developing the project. Together with members of the community, development workers in the NGO sector and UNRWA, as well as the Camp Governance Structure and its Education Committee, the IECCRS Project was constructed around community needs to build the capacity of young emerging leaders within the Rashidieh and El-Buss communities. Three implementing partners were selected: the Women's Humanitarian Organization, Al-Quds Youth Centre and Sour Community Disability Project.

The objectives of the project were based on a shared understanding of the challenges faced by the community: a need for an increased skills base of Palestinian refugee youth to facilitate their entry into the market, youth leadership promotion, as well as capacity building for developing and implementing solutions to community problems. In short, it was an innovative educational training project that had the intention of developing local capacity to mobilize communities in latent conflict to organize their own responses in peak times of crisis.

The project aimed to offer opportunities for learning within a creative environment. Planned activities included English language courses, analytical skills training (including current affairs, debate and internet usage proficiency), community capacity-building workshops (including project cycle management training that focused on identifying and articulating community challenges and presenting proposals to donors) and conflict resolution workshops (mediation and platform design for constructive change).

Stakeholder consultation involved tapping into pre-existing decision-making bodies and key community forums, as well as holding informal discussions over coffee with community members to generate ideas and excitement for the project. Community members expressed a desire to see concrete steps taken with the skills to be acquired through the project, rather than just attend one-off workshops. Most importantly, therefore, the project was to encourage youth to indentify social problems within their communities and develop short- and long-term solutions to these problems, as well as to plan and implement these countermeasures. This project component was to embed a sense of ownership of the youth project through giving beneficiaries the responsibility for project outcomes and increasing their personal stake in its success. The crucial project activity was thus the provision of small-project funding for projects conceived of, managed and implemented entirely by project participants.

The Project Manager described the 'thought process guiding decision-making' as a 'body-up approach', creating a project that would be useful to and sustainable within the community. The project aim was not that the project itself would be sustainable, but that its impact would be.

Potential participants were recruited through placement of advertisements in local community centres and colleges in order to attract youth who were already employed and had completed at least the Baccalaureate II exam. The project aimed to include youth who, while from economically disadvantaged backgrounds, were not traditionally targeted for such projects: those who were already showing an interest in furthering their more-advanced-than-average education and focusing on community work. All interested participants were asked to complete an application form and attend an interview with the Project Steering Committee. The criteria used for participant selection were educational level, current employment and/or academic activities, commitment to the community and willingness to participate in all project components.

A total of 125 applications were received during June and July, 2008, and – at the outset of the first activity – a total of 78 participants were enroled. The average age of participants was 23 years: the youngest being 16 and the oldest 49. The educational background of participants ranged from those who had only completed the Brevet exam and were locally employed, to those who had completed a bachelor's degree and were school teachers. There were 45 participants (66% of whom were female) who completed all project components and received graduation certificates. The decrease in numbers from enrolment to graduation was due to the time constraints of many participants due to work or university, as well as initial misunderstanding of the overall purpose of the project and the time commitment required to successfully complete project components.

The project was managed by a Project Steering Committee made up of the project coordinator, project supervisor, two staff members of NAVTSS, two representatives from the implementing partners, one representative from the Camp Governance Structure and three youth representatives who were identified once the project had started. The youth representatives had to submit an application and then those with successful applications were elected by their peers. The Committee met on a weekly basis to discuss activities implemented and plans for upcoming activities; it also liaised with the community through the same formal and informal channels described above.

A number of project activities encouraged the participation of the community. During the English course, the participants conducted surveys and interviewed community leaders. Two public debates and one mediation showcase were conducted at a local community centre, and the participants organized a presentation of the awareness materials created for their small-group projects. In addition to those who had received formal invitations to attend these public functions, many community members came to show support for their participating family members and neighbours.[3] There was a high level of interaction between participants and the community, and the Steering Committee reported that participants worked hard and presented themselves very well. Project participants stated that this was also the most exciting part of the project, as it allowed participants to publicly demonstrate what they had learned to the community. All beneficiaries felt included and connected with debating and mediation, and felt that the issues they discussed were very closely connected with their experience as refugees.

Box 8.1 Key project strategies

- *Beneficiary consultations as the drivers of the project:* Rigorous monitoring, feedback and adjustment loops were in place throughout the life of the project, including continual participant discussions with the Steering Committee, as well as constant assessment by the trainers of participant interests and needs.
- *Recognition of limitations:* The project was built on the concept of developing leadership capacity of emerging leaders, particularly in community development, based on recognition of the limitations of external agencies to come in and fix the problems in the camp. The project participants needed to develop their skills and self-motivate to address problems themselves, and hopefully continue their community assessment and action after the life of the project.
- *Beneficiary ongoing engagement and stake in the project:* The project design encouraged participants – and by extension their communities – to understand that, while they cannot solve the Middle East conflict by themselves, they can create positive change and solve problems in their immediate environment as a starting point.
- *Addressing needs bottom–up and aligning these with donor priorities:* Through integrating Western approaches with culturally relevant strategies and norms for negotiating dissonance, participants could strategize how both of these could be applied respectfully and successfully within the community structures already in place, and theorize as to what new structures might be useful. The project offered committed young leaders the skills they need to understand existing donor funding frameworks, so that they could continue to seek funding for their own projects.

The Steering Committee was initially apprehensive about the amount of responsibility given to participants throughout the various activities and was worried that the community would not appreciate the new ideas being introduced by the project. However, the Steering Committee's impression of the changes they observed within participants who were able to fully commit to the project was overwhelmingly positive: 'for the participants, the tone, manner and self-confidence with which they approach issues in their lives [personal, professional, communal] has changed, for the better'. Many participants expected that the project would focus more on improving their level of English and computer skills, although some expressed that – since there were so many other components to the project – it was definitely worth the time they had committed. One participant enthusiastically stated: 'I never imagined I would be doing so many amazing things!' Another expressed: 'The most important thing I learned was to be a productive and effective member of my society.'

The Steering Committee felt that participant confidence to communicate and their ability to write in English increased significantly during this project, through giving participants the chance to use the language practically. The Project Evaluation Final Report also found significant improvement in participant command of all the subject areas covered, such as critical thinking, project cycle management, conflict resolution, public debate and mediation.

Box 8.2 Project challenges

- *Sustaining productive community involvement throughout all components of the project*: As the project was implemented over an extended period, maintaining participant momentum was a concern.
- *Balancing the time commitment of participants with their other obligations*: The project required an extensive time commitment; participants, in many instances, were studying and/or employed, leaving little free time for project engagement.
- *Taking into account varying levels of competency in English and educational background*: Managing these disparities was a challenge for the trainers and facilitators.
- *Achieving identifiable results within a limited amount of time:* This was managed through regular community consultations, regular steering group meetings and a thorough final evaluation.
- *Sustaining successes after the conclusion of project activities:* There was uncertainty as to whether a project with such a different approach (in terms of subject matter, practical application and training delivery) would be well received and whether participants would continue to apply the skills learned.
- *Navigating agendas of both community and donor stakeholders within one unconventional project:* This had to be managed through the Steering Committee's constant community and other stakeholder engagement and updates.
- *Keeping the faith while participants developed their skill sets:* Sustaining six months of challenging workshops and activities – all of which required greater commitment than that to which participants were accustomed in a development intervention – meant repeatedly rallying participant spirit when they lost focus or were disheartened by the slow pace of change in their environments.

The small-group projects implemented in the final phase of the project allowed participants to identify problems in the community and articulate both short- and long-term solutions to address them. Each of nine groups identified a community problem, assessed their potential impact on it and created proposal documents for the activities they wished to implement. The documents included a concept note, problem tree, a long-term solution analysis, proposal, a logical framework[4] and budget. Each group then received a maximum of US$1,500 with which to implement their projects, for which they submitted invoices and receipts for all relevant payments. An 'Open Day' was attended by members of the community and representatives of UNRWA, during which each group shared the awareness materials created in support of their projects. These projects are described in more detail in Box 8.3.

Box 8.3 Small-group projects

- *Green Spaces:* This group chose to address environmental and health problems in El-Buss camp through creating a space for people to relax in fresh air.
- *Noise Pollution:* This group addressed the issue of noise pollution in the camps caused by unattended children playing in the streets. The group identified and disseminated information on existing programmes that could occupy the children.
- *Child Labour:* This group created awareness materials – including a video – that highlighted the dangers of employing young children in risky jobs and the negative impact that their dangerous employment can have on the health and well-being of the individual as well as on the community as a whole.
- *Stealing in Schools:* This group developed an awareness campaign to show how stealing affects the security of all children. A UNRWA school decided to continue this campaign throughout the school year.
- *Improving Education:* The problem addressed by this group was the high costs of tutors for students who were not achieving in school. They organized an educational field trip to increase the involvement of parents in their children's education as well as to increase children's level of interest in schooling.
- *Cleaning the Camp:* This group raised awareness on environmental health issues such as unregulated dumping of garbage in El-Buss camp. In addition, they purchased and distributed rubbish bins and bags in which garbage could be classified by type in order to promote recycling and reduction in waste.
- *School Drop-Outs:* This group identified the causes of school drop-out, including teaching quality and the economic and social situation of students, and launched an awareness campaign to draw attention to these issues.
- *Drug Addiction:* This group created posters and brochures concerning the dangers of drug abuse. It also conducted meetings with parents to raise awareness about the risks and social factors that lead youth to become addicted. Furthermore, the group visited drug rehabilitation centres in order to provide support and encouragement to addicts seeking treatment.
- *Food Parcels:* This project distributed food parcels to address the immediate needs of the most vulnerable families in Burj El Shemali camp.

Participants were proud of what they had accomplished, and were happily surprised by the impact they could have within their community. One participant made arrangements to continue the activities of her small project throughout the year in the school where she is a teacher. However, another participant was more cautious, stating: 'The small projects were successful but it is too early to see what impact they may have in the future. The problems were too big to be solved quickly, but we made the first steps.'

The Project Evaluation Final Report found that the project had increased the ability and confidence of participants to make small changes in themselves and their community, quoting some participants saying 'they now feel they are more responsible within their community and that community problems are their responsibility'. About 97 per cent of participant respondents were happy with the problem-solving skills they had learned, reporting that the project had increased their ability to identify, find solutions for and solve problems in the community, though they felt most confident in identifying problems and least confident in solving them.

One member of the Steering Committee expressed that he felt that 'this project has served as a small stone creating ripples in a large pond, the impact of which will increase the more times the project is implemented'. While discussing their role within the community, one participant expressed that 'this project is important for the Palestinians because they face many problems within their narrow environment inside the camp. So this project is important in order for the community to solve problems by themselves in the absence of the power of the government'.

Addendum

Due to the success of the IECCRS Project, funding was secured for a supplementary project that developed both the concept and geographical reach of the original project. The second project took the graduates of the first, and sought to further develop their conflict resolution, mediation, critical thinking, strategic planning and debating skills. A training of trainers was held for the participants of this follow-up project. The group of approximately 25 then developed their own 3-month training courses in either conflict resolution and mediation or critical thinking and debate. They then planned and engaged in outreach and/or conducted trainings in 3 camps and 12 gatherings.

Upon completion of the IECCRS Project, a core group of nine youth established a youth committee in order to continue developing their individual skills and to share these with their community. This youth committee has already prepared a constitution and other founding documents, in addition to beginning their communication and outreach strategies. The committee is in the process of securing funding to obtain training on managing a community-based organization.

Conclusion
Zuki Karpinska

This case study focuses on a particular cross-cutting issue: youth. Through building on the existing skills of high-achieving young persons, the project strengthened the skills necessary for participants to emerge as the new generation of leaders in their communities. By committing to the project, these youth learned to harness their own capacities to identify and articulate community problems, devise possible solutions and apply for the resources necessary to carry out their theories of change. Perhaps most importantly, the participants learned to effectively elicit community debate and garner community support for bottom–up change. All of these skills make the participants more attractive candidates for employment. Perhaps a project like the IECCRS, based on skills development for community activism and leadership, allows participants to create their own opportunities.

This project, despite some participant drop-out, may be classified a success story within youth programming in situations of instability.

> However, due to scarce funding, often a choice must be made between providing primary education and developing prospects for youth. Perhaps because primary education has a clearly defined timeframe, and youth opportunity does not, significantly more funding goes towards primary-age children. (Hollman, 2005: 30)

Yet, a focus on youth may be even more important than that on school-aged children. Young adults are more likely to be recruited into armed forces, sexually exploited or forced to take on dangerous work to contribute to family livelihoods. Lack of quality education and safe employment opportunities may cause frustration, and further the vulnerability of young people. Programmes for young people frequently lack attention to the particular circumstance of youth populations; traditional vocational education (such as carpentry or masonry skills-building) may create a surfeit of trades-people that does not reflect market demand. In essence, lack of attention to the vulnerable and potentially volatile adolescent population may result in conflict that will obliterate development progress.

One of the themes missing from this volume is that of higher education (HE), also known as post-secondary or tertiary education. Little attention is put on the need for post-secondary education opportunities in crisis contexts, other than – usually limited – teacher training. Indeed, the only UN agency with a mandate for HE is UNESCO, which is also one of the least funded. With the average protracted refugee situation lasting seventeen years (UNHCR, 2004: 2), as does the average conflict (UNESCO, 2011: 138), entire generations may be deprived of the opportunity to continue education through the secondary, much less the tertiary, level.

'Tertiary education systems play a critical role in developing the knowledge-intensive skills and innovation on which future productivity, job creation and competitiveness depend in a globalized world' (ibid., 57). How, then, can administrative, financial and sectoral capacity be built within crisis-affected populations in order to effectively absorb and manage international aid? If every additional year of schooling results in a 10 per cent wage increase, how can HE not be considered a prevention measure, as both conflict and disaster are largely fuelled by poverty and inequality? With continued global focus on basic education, from where are capable local leaders to be sprung?

Zeus (2011) strongly challenges three assumptions about HE in refugee settings: that HE is a long-term endeavour, while refugee camps are considered temporary; that a nation-state is required to provide HE; and that traumatized populations dependent on aid lack the capacity to pursue HE. These are clearly fallacious assumptions, as refugee camps may exist for decades; several camps, such as Kakuma in Kenya, have successfully provided distance learning to – admittedly few – refugees (certification is undoubtedly a concern when discussing HE for stateless populations); and the education endeavour has proven – as has affected populations' stated desire for education – to be remarkably resilient. Rather, Zeus argues that HE 'could be a way towards allowing ourselves to see refugees as agents and allowing refugees to be agents of development in having positive impacts on their self-respect and shaping their own as well as their host communities' environment' (Zeus, 2011: 17).

In an article on aid effectiveness in education, Bermingham et al. (2009) write that, more important than easily measurable targets such as enrolment figures or test results, a 'much more important outcome of any education system [is] the extent to which it is helping to nurture confident, creative young people who have the ability and belief to build their countries and make them stronger for future generations' (p. 142). Many aid institutions concerned with education provision in emergencies are, indeed, committed to building leadership in effected communities. However, investments in HE as a percentage of humanitarian aid remain negligible. The mandates of the undisputed institutional EiE leaders, Save the Children and UNICEF, focus on children under 18 years of age. As the prominence of education as a sector of humanitarian aid continues to grow, HE should be an important consideration.

This is certainly not to argue against investments in access to quality primary education, which is a necessary precursor to higher learning. However, greater focus on secondary and tertiary education is fundamental to the sustainability of development and humanitarian aid investments. Widely accepted global frameworks such as the MDGs, which privilege primary education, do a disservice to humanitarian aid action for the full range of educational opportunities, as required by human rights instruments.

Key questions

- What is the utility of incorporating attention to a range of so-called cross-cutting issues in every aspect of programming?
- What is the utility of focusing a project or programme entirely on one cross-cutting issue?
- How does youth capacity building affect their communities?

Notes

1 Dated 1 January 2005.
2 These details are based on informational interviews conducted by the author in 2007 with NGOs in the sector.
3 The information and quotations in this section draw on the *Project Evaluation Final Report*.
4 A monitoring and evaluation tool typically used by aid agencies to track project progress and outcomes.

Further reading

Hollmann, S. (2005), 'Lost generation: the importance of adolescent education in refugee and IDP communities and the barriers to access', in D. Burde (ed.), *Education in Emergencies and Post-Conflict Situations: Problems, responses and possibilities*, Vol. 2. New York: Society for International Education. An article that tackles the same issues presented in this case study: the potential for youth to be a force for change within their communities and in larger development processes.

Yaron, G. (2002), 'Mainstreaming cross-cutting themes in programme and sector aid: the case of environmental issues'. *Natural Resource Perspectives* 77. London: ODI. Retrieved 31 July 2011 from http://www.odi.org.uk/resources/download/2067.pdf.

A brief article explaining how to 'mainstream' one cross-cutting issue – the environment – into sector planning strategies and aid-receiving government budgetary support.

References

Bermingham, D. et al. (2009), 'Aid effectiveness in education: why it matters'. *Prospects 39*, 129–45.

Chaaban, J., Ghattas, H., Habib, R., Hanafi, S., Sahyoun, N., Salti, N., Seyfert, K. and Naamani, N. (2010), *Socio-Economic Survey of Palestinian Refugees in Lebanon*. Report published by the American University of Beirut (AUB) and the United Nations Relief and Works Agency for Palestine Refugees in the Near East (UNRWA).

Hollmann, S. (2005), 'Lost generation: the importance of adolescent education in refugee and IDP communities and the barriers to access', in D. Burde (ed.), *Education in Emergencies and Post-Conflict Situations: Problems, responses and possibilities*, Vol. 2. New York: Society for International Education.

Norway Institute for Applied Studies (FAFO). (2003), *Report on Living Conditions Among Palestine Refugees in Camps and Gatherings in Lebanon*.

Saud, J. (1998), 'The reproduction of political process amongst women activists in Lebanon', in D. Chatty and A. Rabo (eds), *Organising Women: Formal and informal working groups in the Middle East*. Oxford: Berg Publishers.

UNESCO. (2011), *Education for All Global Monitoring Report. The Hidden Crisis: Armed conflict and education*. Paris: UNESCO.

UNHCR. (2004), *Protracted Refugee Situations*. Executive Committee of the High Commissioner's Programme, Standing Committee, 30th Meeting, UN Doc. EC/54/SC/CRP. 14. 10 June. Geneva: UNHCR.

Yaron, G. (2002), 'Mainstreaming cross-cutting themes in programme and sector aid: the case of environmental issues'. *Natural Resource Perspectives* 77. London: ODI. Retrieved 31 July 2011 from http://www.odi.org.uk/resources/download/2067.pdf.

Zeus, B. (2011), 'Barriers to higher education in protracted refugee situations: the case of Burmese refugees in Thailand'. *Journal of Refugee Studies 24*(2), 256–76.

Conclusion 9
Zuki Karpinska

This volume contains stories of advocacy for education as a life-sustaining, life-saving humanitarian response. Central to this advocacy has been aid funding. How to get it and how to spend it, specifically with regard to education in emergencies. As the case studies in this book show, aid agency policies, strategies, programmes and projects are the result of serious consideration of institutional research, individual experience and – ideally – crisis-affected community consultation. Decisions are not made lightly: lives are at stake. Yes, even in the education sector. Although one cannot ethically put a price tag on a life, evidence that a humanitarian intervention could prevent casualties is a powerful advocacy tool vis-à-vis those with money.

The eminent individuals who have contributed to this volume are all interested in, if not devoted to, education as a humanitarian response, as well as education for crisis prevention, crisis mitigation and crisis recovery. They are aware of donor agency commitment to the principles of aid effectiveness (see Chapter 1), and work to design strategies, programmes and projects that offer the most 'bang for the buck'. Every dollar wasted could buy a textbook for populations whose teaching-and-learning materials have been destroyed as a result of violent conflict or natural disaster or for those who have never held a textbook due to crisis-related poverty. Every missed opportunity to strengthen national and local capacity to cope with crisis and provide education opportunities could result in the need for more external aid support.

The argument can be made that – if only one child returns to school or begins their education for the first time after an emergency; if only one casualty is prevented through crisis mitigation measures such as DRR (see Chapter 7) or the sharing of life-saving messages such as hygiene promotion; and if only one traumatized child finds safety, comfort and protection in a learning environment – the intervention is worth the technical and financial resources that it required. And it is difficult to dispute this logic. It is also difficult to prove that an education – rather than a food and water, health or shelter – intervention is the 'best' use of limited aid resources. Ideally, education programming takes place alongside, rather than instead of, the other life-sustaining, life-saving sectoral responses.

Almost every chapter in this volume has described difficult conditions on the ground or in negotiations with policy-makers. Despite these difficulties, aid planners are expected to take into account all of their institutionally mandated accountabilities and 'cross-cutting' concerns (see Chapter 8), and still keep an eye on the goal of increasing access to quality education opportunities for all. However, the authors in this volume seem to have been successful in their endeavours, in their plans 'to do good'. In the education sector. In the mosts challenging of contexts.The authors attest that the relationship between education, aid and aid agencies in humanitarian crises is undoubtedly one characterized by growth, that is, far more funding is available for education as a humanitarian response than at the beginning of the millennium.

The recognition that crisis-affected countries are the least likely to meet the MDGs and EFA targets (see Chapter 1), coupled with the growing recognition that education may be the key to the achievement of all of the MDGs, has hastened a focus on education in situations of instability. These global aid frameworks are almost universally part and parcel of any EiE strategy and programme plan, not only due to donor commitments to these targets, but also as an advocacy message for greater funding for education as a humanitarian response.

The strengthening currency of the term 'fragile states' (see Chapter 3) has focused donor attention on crisis-affected countries and the probability of spillover effects of conflict- and disaster-related poverty. It may sound cynical that Western government representatives are concerned with preventing population migrations into their own countries, with the astronomical cost of peace-building missions or international wars such as those in Iraq and Afghanistan or with the potential insecurity caused by crisis-related poverty and lack of livelihood opportunities. Maybe these are, or maybe these are not, the motivations behind increased funding for EiE. For crisis-affected populations, however, the motivation behind the money that buys blackboards and hope is irrelevant. What is relevant is that the aid comes.

The IASC decision that the education sector warranted its own space within the cluster approach (see Chapter 5) has forced a level of acceptance of education as a first-line humanitarian response from those concerned with the traditional relief sectors of food and water, health and shelter. Successful lobbying on the part of INEE members, especially UNICEF and Save the

Children representatives, has put education firmly on the humanitarian aid map. This achievement and its potential to leverage resources is due to the leadership qualities (see Chapter 4) and dedication of individuals, some of whom have contributed to this volume.

Awareness that humanitarian aid provision by itself cannot prevent countries from reverting to crisis (see Chapter 6) has led to donor acceptance of the need to establish and strengthen in-country capacity to assume responsibility for service provision, requiring extensive education and training for country leaders and even the next generation. Even during the crisis period.

Increasing concern with the inevitable rise of natural disasters due to climate change has opened a debate on the effectiveness of DRR measures, which – again – inherently require education and training to implement. And the corresponding area of concern for conflict-affected populations is the growing attention to the (for now niche) subject of protecting education from attack. The 2011 *Education for All Global Monitoring Report's* insistence that peace and conflict resolution education can help prevent wars (UNESCO, 2011) may instigate attention to such prevention measures, as well. Now we even have our own UN General Assembly Resolution (see Chapter 1), which mentions by name the INEE authoritative handbook (see Chapter 2) on all things education- and crisis-related: the *INEE Minimum Standards.*

Yet, despite all of this growing awareness that education may be essential to the achievement of globally accepted aid goals, the sector is still the poor cousin of humanitarian assistance. Hard evidence of the impacts of education growth is difficult to obtain in the short-term time frame of traditional humanitarian assistance, but hard evidence is what is most likely to win more funding for the sector. Perhaps as short-termism is replaced with a longer-focused into-recovery framework, education will gain prominence. Agencies concerned with education service provision in crisis contexts are also doing themselves no favours by deliberately low-balling education aid needs in donor appeals on the assumption that the lower figure represents what is likely to get funded. Progress has been made, but education is not yet on an equal footing with the other humanitarian sectors of food and water, shelter and healthcare.

We, the EiE professionals who have contributed to this volume (and, hopefully, INEE members all), have helped – each in our own way – to advance the status of education in humanitarian response. Perhaps half a decade from now, there will be no need to advocate for our space within global aid structures. Perhaps it will be easier to get the funding needed to implement our plans 'to do good', to support the provision of life-sustaining, life-saving education services to crisis-affected populations.

Reference

UNESCO. (2011), *Education for All Global Monitoring Report. The Hidden Crisis: Armed conflict and education*. Paris: UNESCO.

Index

Page numbers in **bold** denote figures/boxes.

Abuya, J. 27
Accra Action Agenda, the 9, 13
ActionAid International 27
Active Learning Network for
        Accountability and Performance in
        Humanitarian Action (ALNAP) 71
Adinolfi, C. 21
Adventist Development and Relief Agency
        (ADRA) 42, 43
Afghanistan Basic Education Consortium
        (ABEC) 116, 117, 118
African Development Bank 100
Aga Khan Foundation (AKF) 116, 123
Aguilar, P. 26, 97, 98, 106, 107
Andersen, L. 52
Anderson, A. 7, 19, 25, 87, 103
Anderson, M. 7, 53
Arnhold, N. 15
Asian Development Bank (ADB) 53
Assy, E. P. 93
AusAID 53

Barber, B. 7
Barnett, M. 8
Beall, J. 64
Benefield, P. 15
Benn, H. 55
Bermingham, D. 9, 160
Berry, C. 54
Boston Consulting Group (BCG) 84
Branchflower, A. 53
Brannelly, L. 22
Brock, K. 8, 11

Brown, G. 55, 64
Buchanan-Smith, M. 72, 113
Buckland, P. 17
Buckmaster, J. 65
'build back better' 17
Burde, D. 15, 126
Burmese Migrant Workers Education
        Committee (BMWEC) 41
Bush, K. D. 18

Cameron, D. 64
Carlson, C. 54
Casey, S. 15
Cerna, C. 8
Certificat d'Etude Primaires Elementaires
        (CEPE) 94
Chaaban, J. 150, 151
Chauvet, L. 63
Chelpi-den Hamer, M. 95, 96
Children and Armed Conflict (CAAC) 24
Clarke, B. 74, 77
Clemens, M. A. 12
Colclough, C. 11
Colenso, P. 54, 55, 58
Collier, P. 59, 62
Commitee for Coordination of Services
        to Displaced Persons in Thailand
        (CCSDPT) 38, 41, 43, 44
Community Life Guards (CLG) 139
community-based education and state-
        building (in Afghanistan) 114–26
    ABEC and PACE-A 116–18
    capacity building 122–3

coordination with the ministry of
  education 118–20
 school construction 120
 site selection 124–5
Consolidated Appeals Process (CAP) 12
Cooperative for Assistance and Relief
  Everywhere (CARE) 116
Cornwall, A. 8, 11
crisis prevention (in India) 130–44
 ActionAid's work on DRR 132–5
  in Assam 135–7
  Gramya Vikas Mancha (GVM),
   partnership with 136–7
  integration into curricula 141–2
  integration into the
   community 138–40
  key objective of DRRS Project 140–1
 Sarva Shiksha Abhiyan (SSA) **138**
Crossley, M. 28
Crush, J. 7
Cummings, T. G. 47

Dakar Framework for Action, the 10, 11, 33
Davies, L. 15, 18
De Waal, A. 8
Department for International Development
  (DFID) 25, 85
Devereux, S. 7
Diawara, B. 100
Dickmann, M. 86
Disaster Risk Reduction (DRR) 27, 131
Doise, W. 35
Dolan, J. 83
Dollar, D. 59
Dunant, H. 5

Education Cluster, the 71
Education For All (EFA) 10, 11, 23, 33, 34,
  47, 86, 164
Education For All Fast Track Initiative
  (EFA-FTI) 22

education in emergencies (EiE) 2, 15–18,
  71, 86, 87, 147, 161
 advocacy for 18–21
 current state of 21–4
 two faces of education, the 18
Education pour Tous (EPT) 95
El-Murr, A. 27
Engberg-Pedersen, L. 65
Eriksen, S. E. H. 144
Escobar, A. 51
European Commission, the 22, 53, 56

Flash Appeal, the 12
fragile states 52–4
 DFID's investment 56–8, **56–8**
 DFID's scaled-up support, reasons
  behind 58–65
 MDGs, achievement of 58–61
 peace-building, state-building and
  poverty reduction, processes of 61–4
 UK national interests 64–5
 education in 54–6

Gbagbo, L. 93
Glad, M. 126
Global Cluster Leads 13
Global Coalition to Protect Education from
  Attack (GCPEA) 106
Global Facility for Disaster Reduction and
  Recovery (GFDRR) 144
Goldstein, H. 11
Gordon, P. 109
Greeley, M. 15, 18, 55
Green, A. 63
Groneman, C. 126

Hall, J. 78
Harber, C. 18
Harmer, A. 126
Hazard Safety Cadet Corps (HSCC) 139
Hoeffler, A. 59

Hoffman, J. 102
Hudson, A. 18
humanitarian 6
humanitarian aid 3, 4–6
  aid industry 6–7
  coordination of 13–15
  debates about 8–9
  global aid frameworks 10–13

INEE Minimum Standards 34–7, 148, 165
  original version of **36**
  in the Thailand-Burma border 37–46
  Internal Reflection Tool **40**
Inter-Agency Network for Education in
      Emergencies (INEE) 18, 19, 21, 24,
      25, 34, 55, 87, 130, 164
  agenda of 20
Inter-Agency Standing Committee
      (IASC) 13
Inter-Agency Steering Committee (IASC)
  cluster approach 90–2
  in Côte d'Ivoire 92–110
    coordination mechanisms in 98–105
    education context of 94–6
    GSE, the Cluster and UNICEF in 105–6
    political context of 93
    UNICEF strategy in 96–8
International Rescue Committee
      (IRC) 116
International Strategy for Disaster
      Reduction (ISDR) 131

Jansen, J. D. 11
Jones, S. 59

Kagawa, F. 15
Karen National Union (KNU) 37
Karen Refugee Committee Education
      Entity, the 41
Karpinska, Z. 36
Keck, M. 18

Kirk, J. 15, 18
Kotoglo, K. 59

Laird, S. E. 11
Laub, T. 25
Laurence, C. 54
Leader, N. 54
leadership 71–87
  definitions of 71–2
  Rewrite the Future 84–5
  Save the Children 73–87
Lebanese Civil War 150
Levin, V. 59
Ligon, F. 25
Linden, L. 126
Low, M. 94

Machel, G. 17
  Impact of Armed Conflict on Children 17
McDonald, B. 109
Mackenzie, K. D. 71
Mackinnon, J. 59
McNerney, 118–19, 120, 122, 123, 124
Macrae, J. 7, 126
Maxwell, D. 114
Maxwell, S. 113
Meagher, K. 63
Miguel, E. 62
Millenium Development Goals (MDGs) 10,
      11, 33, 34, 47, 86, 161, 164
Minear, L. 13
MoFA (Dutch) 85
Molteno, M. 76
Moreno Torres, M. 53
Morris, T. 64
Moscovici, S. 35
Mvono, L. 99, 100, 109

National Association of Vocational
      Training and Social Services
      (NAVTSS) 149

National Council of Education Research and Training (NCERT) 142

NGOs 19, 34, 43, 95, 122–3

Nicolai, S. 76, 87

Novelli, M. 10, 12, 24, 64, 65

Nyamu-Musembi, C. 8

O'Dwyer, B. 18

Olsen, G. R. 7

Organization for Economic Cooperation and Development (OECD) 5, 6, 18, 53

Ouattara, A. 93

Panda, D. 27

Paris Declaration on Aid Effectiveness (2005) 9, 13

Partnership for Advancing Community-Based Education in Afghanistan (PACE-A) 116, 117, 118, 123

Perri 6, 7

Piciotto, R. 54

Pigozzi, M. 16

Pizzoni, B. 78

Poole, L. 54

Preston, J. 63

Pureza, J. 64

Putnam, R. 63

Red Crescent Movement 12, 13, 34, 103

Red Cross, the 5, 12, 13, 103

Reindorp, N. 14

Rennie, J. 78

Resodihardjo, S. L. 113

Retamal, G. 94, 97

Richmond, M. 107

Robertson, S. 8

Rose, P. 15, 18, 55

Sachs, W. 7

Saltarelli, D. 18

Santos Pais, M. 92

Saud, J. 150

Save the Children Alliance 21, 101, 161

Schlecht, J. 15

Scott, Z. 61

Second Ivoirian Civil War, the 93

Sen, K. 64

Shanti Volunteer Association (SVA) 42

Sharp, K. 7

Sherrif, A. 47

Sifuni, D. N. 11

Sikkink, K. 18

Simon, D. 7

Sinclair, M. 2, 15, 16

Skinner, D. 78, 80, 84

Slaymaker, T. 54

Slim, H. 6

Sommers, M. 13

Sphere Project, the 34

  Sphere Project Handbook 34, 148

Steets, J. 14

Stewart, F. 63

Stoddard, A. 14, 21

Suhrke, A. 65

Summers, L. H. 47

Taif Agreement (1989) 150

Thevenaz, C. 113

Tomlinson, K. 15

Tove Ramsaas Wang 78, 79, 84

Twigg, J. 131

UNDP 53

Unerman, J. 18

United Nations (UN) 5, 12

United Nations Children's Fund (UNICEF) 10, 18, 19, 21, 71, 72, 73, 85, 99, 100, 101, 103, 104, 161, 164

United Nations Development Programme (UNDP) 10

United Nations Educational, Scientific and Cultural Organisation (UNESCO) 10, 19, 23, 59, 61, 86, 94, 160, 161, 165

United Nations General Assembly 23

United Nations High Commissioner for Refugees (UNHCR) 19, 38, 41

United Nations Mission in Côte d'Ivoire (MINUCI) 98

United Nations Operation in Côte d'Ivoire (UNOCI) 98

United Nations Population Fund (UNFPA) 10

United Nations Relief and Works Agency for Palestine Refugees (UNRWA) 27, 149

United Nations Security Council 24

USAID 53, 73, 117, 123

Vaux, T. 7, 21, 34

Webley, K. 26, 87

Whitbread, J. 84

Wilensky, H. L. 20

Wiles, P. 14

Winthrop, R. 27

World Bank 10, 12, 17, 19, 53, 54, 55, 56, 58, 100, 105, 107, 144

World Health Organization (WHO) 13

Worley, C. G. 47

youth-centred programming (in Lebanon) 149–58

employment and education (among Palestinian refugees) 151

Increasing Employment Capacity and Conflict Resolution Skills (IECCRS) 152–8

political context, the 149–50

Zeus, B. 160